D0200541

MAKING YOUR OWN

JEWELRY

WENDY HAIG MILNE

United States edition published in 1994 by
Storey Communications, Inc.,
Schoolhouse Road, Pownal, Vermont 05261
United Kingdom edition published in 1993 by
New Holland (Publishers) Ltd.,
37 Connaught Street, London W2 2AZ

Copyright © 1993 New Holland (Publishers) Ltd.

Storey Communications, Inc. editor: Deborah Balmuth
Creative editor: Pauline Butler
Art director: Jane Forster
Calligrapher: David Harris
Painted backgrounds: Kathy Fillion Ritchie
Glass backgrounds: Nero Designs

Phototypeset by Ace Filmsetting Ltd, Frome, Somerset
Originated by P & W Graphics Pte Ltd, Singapore
Printed and bound in Singapore by Kyodo Printing Co
(Pte) Ltd.

All rights reserved. No part of this book may be
reproduced without written permission from the
publisher, except by a reviewer who may quote brief
passages or reproduce illustrations in a review with
appropriate credits; nor may any part of this book be
reproduced, stored in a retrieval system, or transmitted in
any form or by any means—electronic, mechanical,
photocopying, recording, or other—without written
permission from the publisher.
The information in this book is true and
complete to the best of our knowledge. All
recommendations are made without guarantee on the part
of the author or Storey Communications, Inc. The author
and publisher disclaim any liability in connection with
the use of this information. For additional information
please contact Storey Communications, Inc., Schoolhouse
Road, Pownal, Vermont 05261.

   Library of Congress Cataloging-in-Publication Data
Milne, Wendy Haig.
      Making your own jewelry/Wendy Haig Milne.
            p.   cm.
      Includes bibliographical references and index.
      ISBN 0-88266-883-8: $18.95
      1. Jewelry making. 2. Beadwork   I. Title.
TT212.M55   1994
745.594'2--dc20
94-4909

      A Storey Publishing Book
      Storey Communications, Inc.
            Schoolhouse Road
         Pownal, Vermont 05261

745.5942
MIL
1994

Contents

Introduction

Throughout history people have adorned themselves with jewelry. The wearing of jewelry represents a powerful symbol of tribal hierarchy, and it has always been used as an ostentatious display of personal wealth. The fashions in jewelry have been as varied as those in clothing; it is fascinating to look in museums, and at books and old portraits to see the styles of jewelry associated with different eras, and to see how looks have evolved and changed.

As a jewelry designer, my own interests lay initially in the field of fine jewelry; in producing pieces in gold and silver using precious and semi-precious stones, enamels, inlays and resins. I became intrigued by craft jewelry, and the scope for creating exciting ideas in this area, after discovering how many beautiful beads, from all over the world, are now available. I found myself working less in the workshop and more on the table and floor at home, inspired by this marvellous variety and the possibilities these beads offered. I was very pleased with my experiments, which were achieved using very basic techniques and equipment.

This book aims to teach basic jewelry techniques, so that the reader can produce each of the projects shown here. Anyone interested in crafts will find this subject

fascinating, as once the first steps are mastered, the techniques can be taken as far as you wish, and you can introduce your own design ideas, color preferences and combinations of materials.

As you use the book you will find that many ideas come from the materials themselves, and that many of these can be found quite close at hand – from shells found on the sea shore, to items purchased from a department store. Once you are looking for materials, an ordinary metal washer may suddenly be seen as a useful component part of a bracelet or necklace, so hardware stores, garden centers as well as

craft shops, will also become a source of inspiration.

Even if you wear little or no jewelry, you can still enjoy making gifts for others, or find the beginnings of what might become a very profitable hobby. It is also very pleasing to be able to re-cycle old or broken jewelry by creating something new and totally original.

I hope that you will find the subject as fascinating as I do, and that this book will be seen as a first step; a springboard for you to discover your own exciting jewelry ideas. I hope also, that it offers you the encouragement to develop new skills.

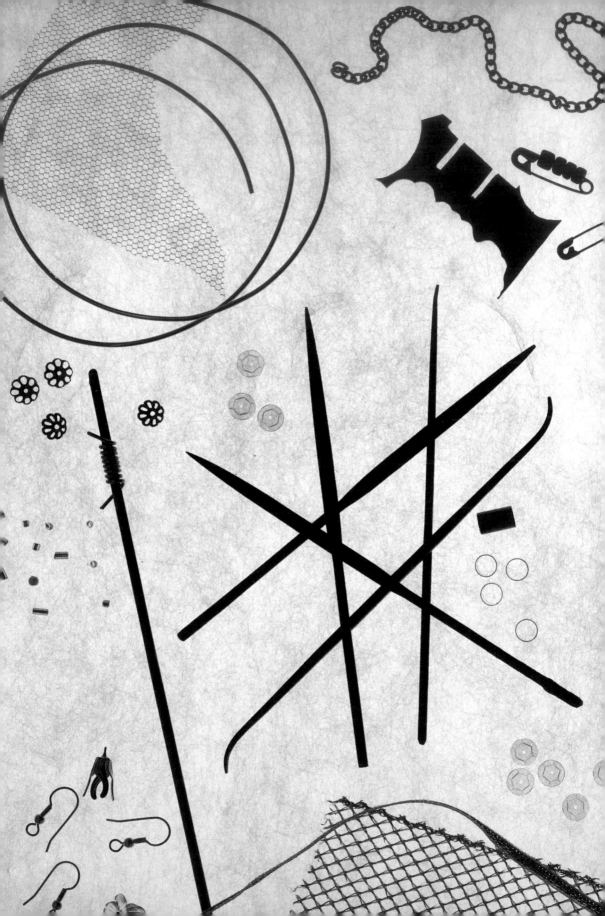

Chapter 1
How to begin

An extensive range of tools and materials are described in this chapter. In case this discourages you from pursuing the subject further, be assured that there are a great many items that can be made with nothing more than beads, wire and a pair of pliers. Obviously the more tools you have, the more techniques you can use, and a wide choice of materials will make a greater variety of design ideas available to you.

In the different projects many basic techniques are repeated. To avoid lengthy explanations each time, the techniques are described in some detail in this chapter, so you can simply refer back to these pages when necessary. You may find that the techniques themselves will make more sense when seen in context, as part of a specific project! Necessary tools and materials are listed for working the techniques, and at the start of each project.

The work area

You do not need to have an elaborate workshop or work bench to start making jewelry. A sturdy table is all that is needed for most of the projects here. However, a special work surface is needed if you want to start drilling, filing and sawing. The ideal is to have a work surface that can be cut and marked without worry. This should be about 1 m (39 in) high and very firmly fixed. A jeweler's work bench is made from thick, solid wood, but for craft jewelry, an old table, providing it is steady, is sufficient.

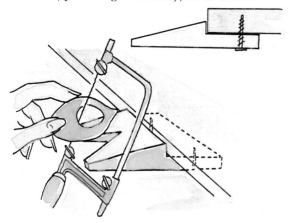

To this you can add a bench pin. This is a wedge-shaped piece of wood which is fixed to the work surface with the sloping side facing upwards. This is invaluable when working on small or intricate items. You

> **Note:** *Measurement conversions from metric sizes are given in 8ths or 10ths of an inch to give the closest accurate conversion.*

will not need this for most of the projects here, but if you go on to more advanced designs you will find it very useful.

The work area must obviously be well lit, and the seat should be comfortable and at the right height for the work surface. If you have a sizeable collection of tools, a magnetic knife rack is handy for keeping them all together. A tool box is practical for storing tools and jewelry components, and a chest of drawers, such as the plastic type sold in hardware stores, is very useful for keeping beads, catches, and other pieces in order.

If you do not have facilities for a separate work area, you will find nevertheless, that you can make the designs work for you by utilizing the available space.

Tools

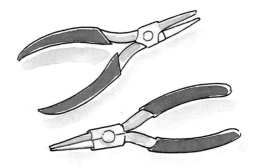

Pliers: These are the most essential tools, and there are three basic types: round nosed pliers, chain nosed pliers and flat nosed pliers. Chain nosed pliers have flattened, gently serrated jaws, and are invaluable, as they are best for gripping wire and opening and closing loops. However, the serration can mark materials if they are squeezed very tightly, so it is advisable to also have round nosed pliers. These pliers have conical jaws which taper to a fine point. Flat nosed pliers, as their name suggests, have a shorter nose than snipe nosed pliers, and the jaws have no serrations.

Inexpensive pliers are readily available, but it is worth buying good quality pliers, as these are precision made and will last.

Wire cutters: Many pliers have a cutting edge, but a separate pair of wire cutters, although not essential, are useful. Diagonal wire cutters or standard side cutters are probably the most practical type for general use, and can be used in most situations.

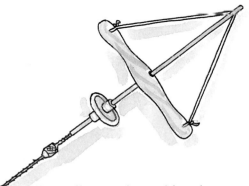

Drills: Drilling can be used for a functional purpose: to provide access for a sawblade, or to make holes as a form of decoration. The part of the drill that does the cutting is called a drill bit, and this is held in place by a chuck, which fits securely over the bit. The drilled hole size depends on the size of bit used. The most practical sizes of drill bit for the projects here are: 0.8 mm (0.031 in), 1.00 mm (0.040 in), 1.2 mm (0.050 in), 1.5 mm (0.060 in), 2.00 mm (0.080 in), 2.5 mm (0.104 in) and 3.0 mm (0.125 in).

The main types of drill used are a bow drill, a hand-needle drill and an ordinary hand or electric drill. A bow drill is a traditional jewelers' drill. It is very easy to control and can be used for a variety of tasks. A hand-needle drill is a small, slim vice drill which jewelers often use with a sharpened broken needle as the drill bit. The drill is twisted with the thumb and first two fingers. The drill end rests in the palm of the other hand, which applies light pressure. Fine thin materials like fragile sea shells can be drilled in this way. A hand or electric drill can be used with larger drill bits to drill through soft stones and wood.

It is wise to drill on a wooden surface so that the drill bit cuts through into a soft surface, to prevent it from blunting. If an item is awkward to hold, you can embed it in plasticine or a re-usable putty adhesive.

Using a bow drill: This drill is controlled with one hand, leaving the other hand free to hold the piece being drilled. As with all drills, the drill bit should slide easily into the chuck. If the jaws of the chuck have to be pushed open, use a larger size chuck.

Mark the position of the hole clearly with a sharp pointed instrument to make an indent, so that the bit fits exactly and will not skid across the surface.

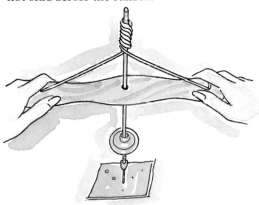

Start drilling slowly by twisting the shaft of the drill, winding the strings around it to pull up the wooden handle. Then rest two fingers on each side of the handle and push it down gently. This will cause the drill to rotate. When the handle has gone right down, it will start to rise as the strings twist around the shaft again. You will soon work out when to apply and when to release pressure to build up speed.

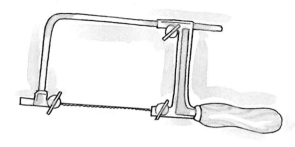

A piercing saw and blades: Using a piercing saw (available from specialist jewelers' suppliers) will open up a range of design possibilities. As with the bow drill, piercing saw skills are soon acquired, although you may have to accept a few broken blades in the early stages! There are two types of piercing saw for the craft jeweler: one has an adjustable frame, and the other a fixed frame. Ideally use a saw with an adjustable frame, as this can be altered to accommodate a shorter length blade, which is useful if a blade end breaks.

The saw frame is made of sprung steel, and this keeps the blade tense, which is necessary for accurate cutting. Saw depths vary, but one that measures 8 cm (3$\frac{1}{10}$ in) is the most convenient. It is wise to start with a size 2/0 or 3/0 when sawing metal. Size 1/0 is better for sawing wood and plastic.

Transferring a design: To prepare a design for cutting out, transfer it to the chosen material (metal, wood or plastic) with tracing paper or ordinary stationers' carbon paper. Trace the design, then draw over the back of the lines with a soft pencil. If you rub the surface of the material with a piece of plasticine, it will leave a surface coating which shows up the traced design more clearly. Place the tracing on the material and draw over the design again, then lift off the paper and score over the design with a sharp point. Alternatively, if you are working with a very simple design, the easiest way to copy it is to glue the tracing on to the material with stick adhesive, then simply saw round the pencil lines.

Using a piercing saw: Fit the blade into the saw with the serrated edge facing outwards, away from the saw, and with the teeth pointing downwards towards the handle. Fasten one end of the saw blade into the blade clamp at the top of the frame, support the frame between the edge of the work surface and your chest, pressing the handle into your chest with the blade clamp

uppermost. Press gently against the wooden handle to flex the saw frame very lightly. At the same time, fasten the other end of the saw blade into the blade clamp and secure tightly with the wing nut. This should ensure that there is enough tension in the blade. You can rub the blade lightly with beeswax to prevent it from sticking to the material when sawing.

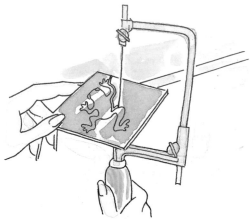

To start sawing, rest the blade against the edge of the material, and draw it down gently. It is the downward stroke that actually cuts, so the full length of the blade should be slowly drawn up each time. Avoid tilting the saw forwards while cutting, as this will cause the blade to break. To turn the corners in a design, keep the blade upright and, while sawing and holding the material firmly in your free hand, gradually turn the frame of the saw.

To cut shapes from the middle of a design you must first transfer the design to the material. Drill a hole within the areas to be cut out, approaching through the waste material. Undo the bottom blade clamp on the saw and pass the blade through the hole before securing the blade once more and checking its tension. Cut round the lines of the design. The more experienced you become, the neater the work will be. Initially you will need to tidy the cut edges with needle files, but with practice the finish may be clean enough to require little further attention.

Tinsnips: If cutting shapes from a large piece of metal, tinsnips or jewelers' shears will simplify the job. Although not essential, they would be useful if you intend doing a lot of metalwork.

Sections of file shapes

Triangular

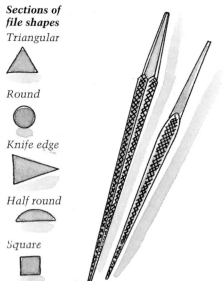

Round

Knife edge

Half round

Square

Files: Files are made in many shapes and sizes to allow jewelers to reach into the most inaccessible areas. They are used to smooth off rough areas, to define shapes and to occasionally file a decorative edge.

You will find both hand files and needle files useful. Practical sizes of hand file are a medium cut (cut 2), a fine or smooth cut (cut 4), and the rough cut (cut 0). The triangular (cut 2) and half round shapes are the most useful sizes of hand file.

A selection of needle files will enable you to work more awkward shapes. The middle length size of 14 cm (5½ in)/cut 2 and the following shapes; round, half round, knife edge and square shapes are the most useful.

Wooden handles can be attached to the tapered points of the files, if you find them uncomfortable to use. When using a file of any type, always file with long strokes for the smoothest finish and accuracy.

Ball-peen hammer: This type of hammer has a head with a flat end on one side and a dome on the other. It is the most useful type of hammer for jewelry making.

Sandpaper (glasspaper): Jewelers use fine grade sandpaper to smooth out marks made by filing, and before polishing. (This is sometimes followed by a substance called water or Ayr stone.) Flour-grade sandpaper is very fine, and gives a good finish, though you can also improve the appearance by hand polishing with polishing compounds after sanding the work.

Polishing compounds: It is not necessary to have a mechanical polisher to buff materials to a lustrous finish. All the designs in this book can be finished with hand polishing. For metalwork, the use of two grades of compound will give a satisfactory finish. These compounds are inexpensive, and are available in block form. However, as little is needed, it may be worth sharing these with someone. The first compound used is a waxy substance known as 'Tripoli' and this is followed with a finer polish called jeweler's rouge for a final sheen.

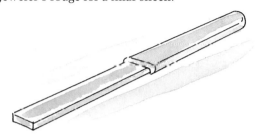

To polish awkward areas, you can make tools by gluing pieces of suede to differently shaped pieces of stick, or by wrapping string round a cocktail stick, or you can simply use a soft cotton cloth. Rub the 'Tripoli' polish on to the sticks (if it seems too dry you can add a little liquid silver polish) and buff over the article. After polishing, wash the article in hot water and detergent to remove all traces of grease before polishing in the same way with the jeweler's rouge. Wash thoroughly again after the rouge polishing. A very soft toothbrush can be used for more intricate pieces.

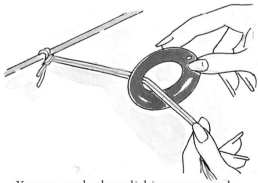

You can apply the polishing compounds to very small cut areas by tying the ends of strings or threads to something steady. Apply the polish, then thread the strings through the hole to be polished and slide the piece up and down the threads to buff.

Materials

Metal wire: An enormous range of gold and silver wire can be bought from precious metal dealers, but this is expensive. However, if you wish to make something special, perhaps using expensive beads, it is well worth the cost. If you are making metal links for example, real silver is preferable. This is because the plating on other metals would eventually be rubbed away with the movement of the links.

Plated wires however, are ideal for making most craft jewelry. Popular diameters of wire are 0.8 mm (0.03 in), 1.0 mm (0.04 in), 1.2 mm (0.05 in), 1.5 mm (0.06 in). These will be all you need for most design ideas. The wires are usually available in set lengths or on a reel. Copper wire of 1.0 mm (0.04 in) or 1.2 mm (0.05 in) diameter is also useful.

Jump rings: These are small metal rings which are used to attach necklace fastenings and to join metal links. As with most component parts in jewelry making, jump rings are available ready-made. However, you can make them very easily to any size required, by twisting wire round a suitably sized forming rod which can be made from a nail, knitting needle or something similar.

Making wire jump rings: Take a length of 0.8 mm (0.03 in) wire and hold it with snipe nosed pliers on the forming rod. Twist the wire closely around the rod until you have as many coils as you think you will need for links or fastenings. Slide this off the rod. Use a piercing saw, to saw along one side of the coil until the rings are all cut through, or cut the rings away with wire cutters. You can then neaten the edges of the rings with a fine hand file if required.

Metal: Metal is available in sheet and wire form. Silver sheet is ideal for jewelry as it is relatively malleable and will not tarnish quite as easily as brass or copper. You can also varnish a metal surface to prevent tarnish. Thin sheet of 8 b.m.g (25 gauge U.S.A.) is easily pierced with a 02 or 03 sawblade.

Brass curtain hoops are useful for making links or earrings. You can also hammer them flat to create an attractive beaten gold effect.

Findings: As you begin to collect beads, shells and other interesting materials, try to visit craft shops to gather 'jewelry findings'. These are the headpins, eyepins, catch fastenings, brooch and earring fittings; all usually available in gold or silver, which you will need to complete your projects, as well as cord, thread and leather thong.

There are addresses of suppliers at the back of the book who supply a selection of jewelry findings. Ideally, try to visit a

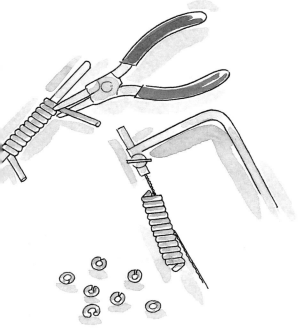

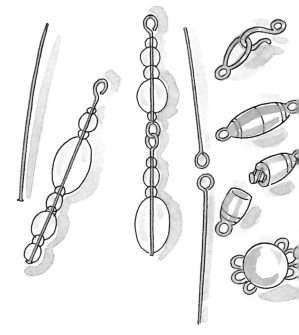

supplier so that you can see the choices available, although shapes, sizes and colors are usually clearly indicated in the catalogues. Most findings are available individually or in pairs, but it is more economical to buy them in quantity.

Headpins and eyepins: Headpins are long wires with a flattened end. They have many uses as well as being the basic component for bead earrings, and for attaching beads to anything you are making. Headpins are usually available in 3.8 cm (1½ in), 5 cm (2 in) and 7.6 cm (3 in) lengths.

Eyepins are similar to headpins but they have a loop at one end instead of a flattened end. Eyepins are used between two other component parts, and are looped on to each. They may be used to lengthen a pair of earrings by attaching a beaded eyepin between the beaded headpin and the ear fitting.

Headpins and eyepins are occasionally stocked in two different diameter sizes. Always check that the holes in the beads fit the pins easily, and are not so large that the beads slip off the pin.

Catches: Used for necklaces and bracelets, these fastenings range from simple hook clasps and bolt rings to screw catches and very ornate diamanté boxes. Usually large pieces of jewelry look better with a strong, suitably sized clasp, and delicate designs look better with a small screw catch or a hook clasp and jump ring. Most catches have a loop at each side, making it simple to attach to the item of jewelry. Multiple loop and triple link catches are also available for necklaces and bracelets which are made up from several strings.

Bell caps: These are used to cover the ends of cords, and as an end to multiple string necklaces and bracelets, or as the tops of multiple drop earrings. The strings or wires are attached to an eyepin, and this is passed through the cap so that the loop and ends are hidden inside. The straight end of the eyepin is then twisted into a loop on the top of the cap, and this is attached to a fastening clasp or earring fitting.

Crimps: These are used to secure the ends of necklaces and bracelets before they are attached to the clasp. Cord and lace crimps are designed to squeeze on to the end of cord or lace placed between the crimp's open sides. The loop on the crimp is then fixed to a bolt ring or clasp directly, or with a jump ring. Calotte crimps are cup shaped, and designed to fold over the knot at the end of bead thread or nylon gut. The knot is placed in the cup so that the thread sits securely inside the crimp when it is closed. Crimps are all squeezed shut with pliers.

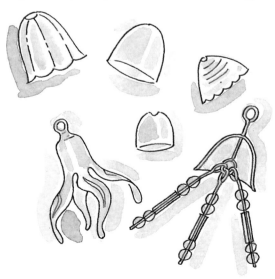

Gimp: This is a length of very fine coiled wire. It is used for the ends of threaded beads as an alternative to the calotte crimp. Gimp is usually available in 5 cm (2 in) lengths. The thread is passed through the gimp, which is then passed through the loop on the clasp before the thread is tied back on to itself.

Earring fittings: The range of these fittings is so wide that there is not room to describe them all. Wide choices are available in both clip-on and hook styles. There are flat fittings which can be glued directly on to the backs of earrings, flat styles which accommodate loops for drops, and there are perforated discs for use with beads. When selecting a fitting consider the overall weight of the earrings, and which style would allow the design to 'sit' well.

Earring hoops are very easy to make with wire, but they can be bought in both round and oval shapes in a variety of sizes. They are simple to use, and are a good starting point for beginners working with beads, as these are also easy to use.

Brooch fittings: Most brooch fittings for the craft jeweler consist of a flat brooch bar with pin and revolving or hook catch. The fitting is usually glued to the back of the item. There are also ornate perforated discs, for use with beads. Headpins and eyepins can be attached to this style of fitting, to create elaborate drops from the brooch unit.

Lapel pins look like large headpins. They are made from thick wire, with one flattened end and a safety end to cover a sharp point. They can be made into ornate hat pins or bent double to make bar brooches, with the flattened end shaped to form a hook.

Bead cups: These are small filigree caps that can be placed over the holes in beads to make a more elaborate looking unit. They are available in a variety of colors and sizes to fit most beads.

Other findings: Different styles include cufflink backs, tie pins, hair clips, shoe clips, bells, coins, chains and lots of fun-shaped drops which include hearts, arrows, fish, flower shapes and other novelties.

Beads: The history of beads is fascinating, and there are many books on the subject. Start a bead collection by asking friends and family for discarded, old or broken necklaces, and search for them in second hand shops and sales, as beads can be bought quite cheaply from these sources. Look carefully, as occasionally some exceptional beads can be found in otherwise unremarkable strings. Remember too, that bead cups can be used to decorate plain designs.

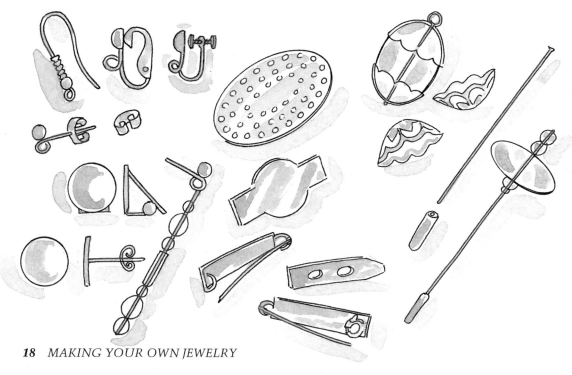

Wooden beads are available in a wide range of colors, shapes and sizes, and these can be stained and decorated in a variety of ways. Unusual handmade beads can be bought from suppliers, and these beads range from simple designs in wood, clay and papier mâché to beautiful, exotic designs in glass, hand painted ceramics and inlaid silver and bone designs. Look for unusual shapes, and for adaptable tubular beads, washers and drops.

Small metallic beads are also useful as they can add sparkle to a design, and the small glass beads known as rocaille ('little rocks') find a place in almost all beaded designs. Other very small, useful beads include tubular bugle beads.

When you plan your piece, try to buy a few extra beads each time, and in this way you will add to your collection.

Stones: Smooth, tumble-polished stones can be bought with or without drilled holes. Drilled stones can be used for pendant drops and earrings, or to hang from brooches and bracelets. Stones without holes can be encased in wire 'cages' or tied with leather or twine, and linked together. Slate and sandstone are soft stones, and these together with agate slices, which often have a natural hole in the middle, can also be drilled. Small slices of agate look very striking as drops, or set into beaded necklaces.

Shells: Exotic shells, as well as common varieties, can be bought from specialist suppliers, but you can gather a good basic collection of shells from the sea shore.

Collect spirals like whelks and winkles, limpet cones, domed-shaped cockles, rounded cowries, flat donax shells and long pointed turitellas. The delicate colors of mother of pearl, and the bright iridescence of abalone shell are well known, but lovely colors also occur in more common shells. To clean shells, use an old toothbrush with detergent and hot water. They can then be waxed or varnished.

Drilling holes in natural forms: It is easy to drill holes in many shells, and some can be pierced with a strong needle. For thick shells (or horn and bone or beans and pulses), use a bow drill or a hand-needle drill with a 1 mm (0.04 in) size bit. The hole size can be increased by working it with a round nosed needle file.

Stones vary considerably, but sandstone and slate can be drilled with an electric drill and a 3 mm (0.125 in) diameter masonry bit. When drilling through shells and stones avoid working very close to the edge, as the material may chip or splinter.

Wood: Scraps, with their various grain patterns and shades, can suggest a variety of uses. Very thin smooth slices are the most

ALBUQUERQUE ACADEMY
LIBRARY

suitable as these are easy to cut with a piercing saw and a number 1 blade.

Wooden beads and curtain rings are versatile, and these have been included in a number of projects in this book.

Painting wooden beads and rings: Small pots of enamel paints and varnish are ideal for creating 'faux' effects like marbling, or for sponging and stippling textures on large craft beads and wooden curtain rings. Use fine and medium-sized artist's brushes, and always clean them immediately after use.

It is easiest to paint or varnish beads if they are held securely on a rod; a knitting needle or skewer is ideal, as this can be turned as you paint. Suspend another rod between two level objects, and when each bead is finished, transfer it to this rod and leave it to dry. When working on a group of beads, you may find that as the last bead is added to the drying rod, the first bead may be dry enough for a second color. Always let each coat of paint dry thoroughly.

To work special paint effects, first paint the beads with a base color. When this is dry you can continue as desired. For marble effects, look at a real piece of marble or onyx for inspiration, then use a very fine brush or a feather to create the 'marble' veins. To sponge-paint use small pieces of fine make-up sponge to create subtle patches of color, and for stippled effects use an old toothbrush to apply tiny pin points of color – strongly contrasting colors create depth, while two or three shades of metallic paint can produce a lovely beaten metal effect.

To paint curtain rings, paint one side at a time, and leave them to dry flat before turning them and painting the other sides.

Plastic: Various types of plastic can be recycled for jewelry designs, including clear sheet plastic and the rigid plastic used to create 'bubble' packs. These can be used to laminate fabric and paper to make earrings and brooches.

Old plastic beads, particularly the interesting styles from the 1950s and '60s, are also worth collecting. As with all character beads, these can be used on their own or mixed with other varieties.

'Friendly plastic': This is one of the newest mediums in the craft market. It is sold in short strips in a range of bright rainbow colors and iridescent effects. When heated the plastic is exceptionally pliable, so it can be molded by hand or cut to shape with scissors. To work with the plastic, you first warm it in hot water or in an oven. If the result is not as desired, the plastic can simply be reheated and remodelled. (Full instructions are provided by the manufacturer.) You can also use this plastic to cover wooden rings and beads.

Leather thong, colored cord and threads:
Leather thong is available either flat or round and in a wide range of colors. To avoid waste it is preferable to buy thong by the metre (yard) rather than as pre-cut lengths. The round thong is available in small, 2 mm (0.08 in) and 1 mm (0.04 in) diameters, but you may find a restricted color choice in these sizes. Lace crimps will fit the ends of round thong.

Colored laces and cord are excellent for large beads and those with large holes, especially for wooden beads. Look in notions departments and craft suppliers for different sizes and types of cord.

Thread is needed for smaller size beads, and those with small drilled holes. Various threads are available for extra strength, including nylon monofilament (fishing line gut) and plastic coated wire (tigertail).

A wide choice of colors in polyester cotton thread or pearlized silk thread can also be used for traditional threading and knotting between beads. If you are using valuable beads it is well worth the effort of knotting between each bead. This is to reduce the friction caused by beads rubbing together, and also as a safeguard against the thread breaking; if this should happen only one bead would fall loose.

Elastic is useful for making bead bracelets and choker necklaces. Decorative gold and silver elastic thread can be used for threading lightweight beads, but for heavier beads use thicker, round elastic.

Threading beads: When threading narrow drilled beads use a threading needle. Make one yourself by twisting very very fine wire into a needle length, leaving the looped end open. Tie a knot at the end of a double thread and enclose it in a calotte crimp, or pass the thread through a gimp and push it to the end of the thread (leaving sufficient thread for tying). When knotting thread, dab some glue or clear nail varnish on to the knot to secure it, and leave it to dry.

The knot between each bead should be large enough to prevent it slipping into the bead. A single knot on a doubled thread is usually adequate, but on a single thread, pass the thread twice through the loop of the knot if necessary, and draw it up close to the bead.

Fabrics: Unusual fabrics and ribbons, particularly those with metalized threads and finishes, are very versatile. They can be laminated between layers of clear plastic, or used to cover base shapes.

The hunt for fascinating items becomes very engrossing, and you can quickly acquire a collection of 'useful materials' which will prove invaluable in jewelry making!

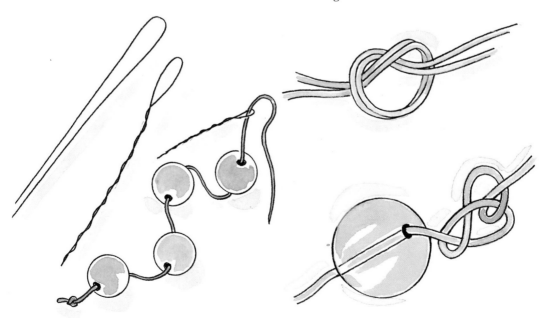

Chapter 2
Earrings

Earrings are one of the most popular types of jewelry. With so many styles to choose from – studs, drops and hoops, and an infinite variety in each category – there is something for everyone. Many of the designs in this chapter use fashionable, bold shapes and show tribal and ethnic influences, but most of the designs can be modified to suit your style.

Bead drops and hoops

Earrings using drop or hoop shapes are quite easy to make, particularly as so many component parts are available to help with design. Earring kits are increasingly available from craft suppliers, and you will find these useful, as they show clearly how to make a variety of designs.

REQUIREMENTS

Earring hoops with tubular sockets and loop fittings; in various sizes and metal finishes, (or make hoops from 0.6 mm (0.025 in) or 0.8 mm (0.031 in) diameter wire)
Headpins and eyepins in various lengths, and metal finishes (or from wire as above)
Earring fittings; studs and backs, fish hook earwires, earclips or earscrews
Beads and metallic beads and 'liquid' silver or gold finish tubes
Thin ribbon for bows
Round nosed pliers, snipe nosed pliers, wire cutters
*(See the **How to begin** chapter pages 12 to 23 for information on tools and materials.)*

Making eyepins and hoops:

Many sizes of these are available, but eyepins and hoops can easily be made from gold and silver colored wire. Choose wire in a size to pass through the holes in your beads so that they fit comfortably, without the wire sticking or the holes gaping.

To make an eyepin, simply bend the end of a wire length into a loop, then cut off the required length, leaving sufficient to bend the other end into a loop. Bend this into

shape, making sure both loops are even.

Make a collection of hoops by winding a length of wire round a cylindrical shape of the required size. (Use a broom handle or similar.) Cut the hoops from the wire. Thread the beads on one end of the wire hoop, and bend the other end into a loop. Twist this round the first end, and attach the first end to an earring hook or stud.

Blue glass drops with tartan bows

Bows can be used to complement the color of beads. Make them yourself, and secure the knot with a dab of glue, or buy ready-made bows from notions departments.

REQUIREMENTS

Two blue glass beads 16 mm (⅝ in) diameter
Two small tartan bows to match beads
Six silver beads 5 mm (³⁄₁₆ in) diameter
Four dark red rocaille beads 5 mm (³⁄₁₆ in) diameter
Two silver fish hook earwires (or preferred fittings)
Two silver headpins 5 cm (2 in)
Two short silver eyepins

Making the earrings:

1 Start with the silver beads, and pass one on to each headpin. Follow with a large blue glass bead, then add a silver bead, a dark red bead, a silver bead, and a dark red bead. Use the round nosed pliers to twist the end of the headpin into a loop and cut off any excess wire.

Opposite: *Earrings from top to bottom: blue glass drops with bows, frosted glass drops, pink beaded drops, 'antique' brown bead drops, and hoops decorated with small beads.*

Six pink glass rocaille beads
Four 5 cm (2 in) silver headpins
Two short silver headpins
Two silver earring fittings (bead loop and
earring back)
Round nosed pliers, wire cutters, a pencil

2 Pass the eyepin through the tartan bow, piercing the knot at the center. Twist the top of the eyepin into a loop and trim to neaten with wire cutters.

3 Attach the bead drop to the loop under the tartan bow, and fit a fish hook earwire to the eyepin loop on top of the tartan bow. Ensure that the neatest side of the bow is showing to the front.

Pink beaded drops with twisted wire

These pretty earrings have the added interest of a twisted wire running through the design. A heavier wire could be used, or one with a different color finish to complement your choice of beads.

If made in cream and white beads, these earrings are delicate enough to choose as bridal jewelry. They could be made to match the beading on the wedding gown.

REQUIREMENTS
Two pink pearl beads 10 mm (⅜ in)
  diameter
Two frosted drilled flower beads 15 mm
  (⁹⁄₁₆ in) wide
Two frosted button back beads 10 mm
  (⅜ in) wide
Four pink crystal beads 5 mm (³⁄₁₆ in), two
  slightly darker
Eight pearls 3 mm (⅛ in) diameter

Making the earrings:
1 Take two of the 5 cm (2 in) headpins. Pass a pearl on to each one. Add a pink pearl and another pearl.

2 Take the shorter headpins and pass each through the hole in a drilled frosted flower bead. Twist the wire into a loop at the back of the flower and cut off the excess. Pass each flower on to a beaded headpin. Follow with the button back flowers.

3 Take the other 5 cm (2 in) headpins and cut the flat ends off. Using the pencil, twist each headpin round the pencil to make a loose coil. Slide the wire from the pencil and, using the round nosed pliers, twist one end of each coil on to a beaded head pin.

4 Add the other beads to the beaded headpins in the following order: pearl, rocaille, darker pink crystal, rocaille, pearl, rocaille, lighter pink crystal. Place the other loop at the end of the headpin coils on to the beaded headpins after the last bead. The coils should twist round the beads. Twist the end of each beaded headpin into a loop and attach an earring fitting.

Variations:

Frosted glass drops have a lovely, cloudy appearance. Because these beads are heavy it is best to limit the number of beads, and use interesting shapes like these flat washer shapes and oval beads for impact. 'Liquid' silver tubes threaded on to the headpins give length to the design.

'Antiqued' brown bead drops are complemented by gold wire fittings. Matching drops and round beads are set off to advantage by toning horn washers.

Hoops with gold bead and crystal drops

Although large, these hoops appear delicate because of the fine wire and the light, clear crystal beads.

REQUIREMENTS
*Two 40 mm (1⁹/₁₆ in) gold earring hoops
    with socket and loop fittings
Two gold headpins 5 cm (2 in) long
Four gold headpins 3 cm (1⅛ in) long
Four gold beads 5 mm (³/₁₆ in) diameter
Eight gold beads 4 mm (¹/₅ in) diameter
Sixteen gold beads 3 mm (¹/₈ in) diameter
Twelve crystal beads 7 mm (¹/₄ in) diameter
Eight amber glass rocaille beads
Two gold ear hooks
Round nosed pliers, wire cutters*

Threading the beads:
1 Start by beading the headpins as follows: To the longer headpins add first a 4 mm (¹/₅ in) gold bead, followed by a crystal, a rocaille and a 4 mm (¹/₅ in) gold bead.

   To the shorter headpins add first a 4 mm (¹/₅ in) gold bead, then a crystal, a rocaille and a 3 mm (¹/₈ in) gold bead. With the pliers, twist the end of each headpin into a small, equal size loop.

2 Take the earring hoop and add the beads and headpins as follows: one 5 mm (³/₁₆ in) gold bead, one 3 mm (¹/₈ in) gold bead, a shorter looped headpin, a 3 mm (¹/₈ in) gold bead, a crystal, a 3 mm (¹/₈ in) gold bead, a long looped headpin, a 3 mm (¹/₈ in) gold bead, a crystal, a 3 mm (¹/₈ in) gold bead, a shorter looped headpin, a 3 mm (¹/₈ in) gold bead and finally a 5 mm (³/₁₆ in) gold bead.

Assembling the fittings:
1 Close each hoop by pushing the open end into the socket, and squeeze gently with pliers to hold the wire firmly in place.
2 Attach an ear hook fitting to the small loop on top of each hoop.

Hoops with patterned clay drops
These Peruvian clay drops are enhanced by the use of small colored beads chosen specially to match the richly patterned clay drops.

REQUIREMENTS
*Gold earring hoops 25 mm (1 in) diameter
    with socket and loop fittings
Two gold headpins 5 cm (2 in) long
Two patterned clay bead drops 2.5 cm (1 in)
    long
Ten large black rocaille beads 5 mm (³/₁₆ in)
    diameter
Six large red rocaille beads 5 mm (³/₁₆ in)
    diameter
24 gold beads 3 mm (¹/₈ in) diameter
Two gold bead, loop and back earring
    fittings (or as preferred)
Round nosed pliers, wire cutters*

Making the earrings:

1 Start by beading the headpins as follows: Pass on first a small gold bead, followed by the patterned clay drop, a gold bead, a red rocaille bead, a gold bead, a black rocaille bead and a gold bead. Twist a loop at the end of the headpin close to the last bead, and cut off any excess wire if necessary.

2 Bead the open hoops by passing them on in the following pattern: gold bead, black bead, gold bead, red bead, gold bead, black bead, gold bead. On to each hoop pass on the loop of a patterned clay drop, and continue beading the hoop to match the beads on the other side.

3 Close each hoop by pushing the open end of the wire into the socket, and squeeze gently with pliers to hold the wire firmly in place. Add the earring fittings to the loops.

Variations:

Large beaded hoops with center drops can be made by attaching a beaded headpin to the hoop wire as it passes through a socket and loop fitting. To do this, first bead the headpin and loop the end. Bead the hoop as desired, then hold the loop of the beaded headpin between the two tubular sockets of the hoop fitting, and simply push the hoop wire right through the headpin loop. Squeeze the socket closed with pliers.

Double hoop earrings like this silver and pearl beaded design are also worked by attaching the central hoop to the outer hoop wire as it passes through the socket fitting. Here the two hoops are joined with a simple jump ring.

Long tube drops are effective at the center of small beaded hoops. These drops are actually the ends of 'shoe string' ties – the kind of tie made from leather or cord thong. You can glue a bead into the wide, open end of the unit, and glue an eyepin into the narrow end. Secure this with pliers.

Lace bobbin earrings

Wooden lace making bobbins have changed very little in appearance over the years. They often have a fine drilled hole at the top, through which decorative hoops of beads can be added. Here the bobbins are painted to complement their shapes, and the beading holes are used for earring fittings.

REQUIREMENTS
Wooden lace bobbins in matching pairs
Wires 0.6 mm (0.125 in) or 0.8 mm (0.03 in)
*   in different finishes; silver or gold, copper*
*   or colored fuse wire*
Enamel paint and varnish
Small size craft paint brushes
Pliers and wire cutters, flat surface needle
*   file*
Instant bonding glue or epoxy resin
Earring fittings
*(See the **How to begin** chapter pages 12 to*
*   23 for information on tools and*
*   materials.)*

Wiring the bobbins with loops:

Take a piece of wire and thread it halfway through the hole in the bobbin. Dab a little glue to hold this end in place. Bend the wire over the top of the bobbin, and bend it round to form a loop on the top. Twist this loop round once, then bend the wire back round to the other side of the drilled hole. Cut off the wire so that there is just enough to glue halfway through the hole as before. Attach the earring fitting, and glue the wire.

Drilling a bobbin:

If working with an undrilled bobbin, you can make a hole at the top to hold an earring fitting. Use the correct size of drill bit to suit the wire. Drill 5 mm (³/₁₆ in) into the wood. Twist the wire into a loop and peg shape, and glue the peg into the hole.

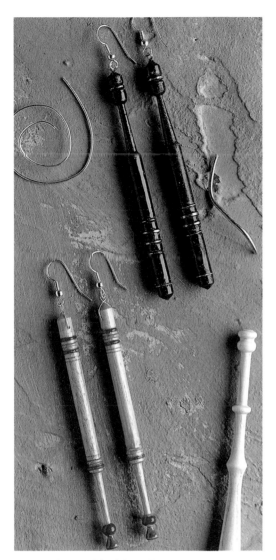

Traditional lace bobbins make attractive drop earrings, especially when painted or decorated with colored wires.

Making the earrings:

1 Start by twisting the colored wire round the bobbin in one of the carved grooves. Cut the wire so that the ends butt-join. Use this piece to measure and cut three red wire hoops and two green hoops for each earring.

2 Use the pin to 'draw' some glue round the first bobbin groove, and use the pliers to hold the colored wire tightly round the groove. Repeat with the other wires, aligning all the butt-joins on one side.

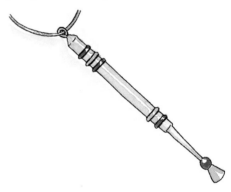

Natural wood bobbin drops

Wrap colored plastic coated wire round the bobbin grooves, then add painted details to accentuate the bobbin shapes.

REQUIREMENTS

Two wooden lace bobbins 9.7 cm (3³/₁₆ in) long

Red and green plastic coated wire, cut to fit round bobbin diameter

Silver wire 0.8 mm (0.03in) diameter, 6 cm (2⁴/₁₀ in) length

Red and green enamel paint, varnish and fine brushes

Silver earring fittings

Pliers and wire cutters

Instant bonding glue and a pin or needle

3 Once all the wires are in place, cut the silver wire into two 3 cm (1²/₁₀ in) lengths, and make a top loop through each bobbin hole. Suspend each bobbin by its loop ready for painting.

4 Paint the ends of the bobbins with red and green paint, and allow to dry. When the paint is dry, varnish each bobbin and allow them to dry completely. Attach an earring fitting through each loop.

Variations:

Painted bobbins and metal wire are another design option. Here copper and silver wires add some sparkle to the long drops.

Laminated plastic

You can re-cycle waste packaging and scraps of patterned fabrics and papers to make these earrings. Look for rigid plastic with perfectly flat surfaces; this is often found in toy packaging. Cut out all the usable pieces and store them flat. Metalized fabrics, ribbons and foils, as well as gift wrapping paper, are all ideal materials for these unusual jewelry designs.

REQUIREMENTS
Flat rigid plastic
Fabric or ornate paper
Instant bonding glue
Scissors
Gold enamel paint and fine paintbrush
Glue-on earring backs, or jump rings and hanging earring fittings
(See the How to begin chapter pages 12 to 23 for information on tools and materials.)

Laminating material between plastic:
Cut attractive scraps of fabric or paper into matching pairs of shapes. Try bold geometric shapes like squares, circles and triangles, and shapes that will overlap, to create interest. Cut two pieces of plastic (plates) for each earring, slightly larger than the material, to allow a 2 mm (¹⁄₁₀ in) border all round.

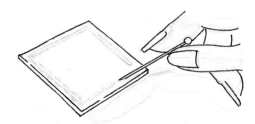

   Take the back plate of plastic and spread a little glue in the middle and round the edges; you can run the glue round the edges of the plastic with a pin, to avoid it marking the material. Place the material centrally over this. Put the front plate on top and press gently round the edges to bond.
   You may find that the glue affects some materials adversely. If this happens, glue round the plastic edges only. Other materials tolerate glue applied on both sides, so with these you can omit the outer plastic border. Experiment with scraps.

Attaching earring fittings:
The most simple way is to glue a flat earring fitting to the back of the plastic shape. Alternatively you can drill a hole near the top of the earring and attach an ear fitting to this with a jump ring.

Tartan ribbon earrings
You could make these earrings to match another accessory made from the same tartan. The gold threads running through the ribbon balance well with the gold border. The design could also be adapted easily to make shoe or hair ornaments.

REQUIREMENTS
Length of tartan effect ribbon or paper ribbon
Piece of rigid clear plastic 7 cm (2¾ in) square
Gold enamel paint and paintbrush
Sharp scissors and ruler
Flat plate earring fittings
Instant bonding glue

Making the earrings:
1 Divide the clear plastic into four quarters with the ruler, and mark the dividing lines on the plastic with a sharp point. Cut out the squares with scissors. From the tartan ribbon cut two equal squares, just slightly smaller than the plastic squares.
2 Glue the tartan in place on the back plates, and fit the front plates over. Leave to dry, then paint round the edges of the front plates with gold paint. This will give a finished look, and cover any glue marks.
3 Using the instant bonding glue, attach the earring fittings to the back plates. For large shapes, glue them near the top, rather than at the center, to prevent the earrings from leaning forward when worn.

Gold and silver triangles
Use craft ribbon to make these earrings. On one side of the ribbon the threads appear gold, and on the other side silver. Copy this effect, or substitute foil papers. Lace fabrics or silk are other alternatives.

REQUIREMENTS
Length of open weave ribbon
Piece of rigid plastic 7 cm (2¾ in) square
Sharp scissors and ruler
Flat plate earring fittings
Instant bonding glue

These earrings are made from clear plastic sheeting mounted over scraps of fabric, ribbon or giftwrapping paper. Glittery materials and simple geometric shapes create simple, but eye-catching effects.

Making the earrings:

1   Divide the clear plastic into quarters, mark the lines with a sharp point and cut out. Divide and cut the squares diagonally into triangles.

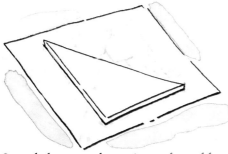

2   Spread glue over the entire surface of four of the triangles. Place a length of ribbon over these four shapes and press to stick. (As one edge of this type of ribbon is stitched, holding all the threads in place, it is best to cut it to size round the edge of the plastic, after gluing.) Add more glue if necessary and press the top plastic triangles in place.
3   Take two of the triangles and glue them together – one with the gold side upwards, and one with the silver side upwards.

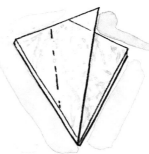

Overlap the triangles slightly so that they meet at one corner, and both colors of thread are clearly visible. Cut off one of the pointed corners to create an irregular shape.
4   Assemble the other earring in the opposite combination, so that one earring has a gold top triangle, and the other a silver triangle. Remember too, to keep the earring shapes as mirror images of each other. Glue earring fittings near to the top of the backplate.

Variations:

Geometric drop earrings are made by linking two different sized laminated squares together with three jump rings. Choose a metal color to complement the material – in this case sparkly foil giftwrap.

Curved shapes are also easy to cut with scissors. Here a textured cream and gold paper is matched with a gold painted border.

Paste jewel drops and studs

Paste jewelry is a general term used to describe all kinds of imitation stone. Some of these, such as antique paste, are collectors items and are quite expensive, while others cost very little. The manufacture of sophisticated, synthetic stones has made it difficult to tell a fake from a genuine stone – particularly since fake stones are now being manufactured with 'flaws'.

The paste stones used here are inexpensive glass or plastic, but they still look good as big and bright fun earrings.

REQUIREMENTS
*Paste stones, beads and drops in a variety of
    shapes and colors*
*Flat plate earring backs, some with a hoop
    for drop styles*
Headpins and eyepins in gold and silver
Bellcaps in gold and silver
Jump rings
Triple loop rings
*Backplates with loops or drilled holes or
    flat drops with loop*
Instant bonding glue
Round nosed pliers and wire cutters
(See the **How to begin** *chapter pages 12 to
    23 for information on tools and
    materials.)*

Gluing bellcaps to drop stones:
The easiest type of cap to use is an open one with claws which open to fit whatever drop bead or paste stone you are using. These types of bellcaps are available in various sizes to fit large or small drops. Apply the glue sparingly to the inside of the claws, to prevent any excess seeping visibly on to the stone when the claws are squeezed closed.

Triple loop links:
These are used for triple string necklace fastenings, but they can also be used to create attractive drop earrings. The top part of the earring is joined to the single loop at one end of the fitting, and the triple loops are used to suspend drop beads.

Backplates:
If you wish to use a flat backed stone without a drilled hole as an earring drop, you will have to glue it to some kind of backplate that has a loop.

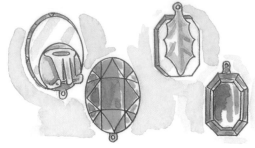

You can use metallic drilled shapes for this and, as some of these are available as rather attractive shapes such as leaves, they can also be featured on their own.

A flat backed stone used at the top of an earring can simply be glued to the fitting.

Triple drop paste stone earrings
Despite their appearance, these ornate earrings are quite simple to make. They can be changed into a bolder, heavier looking design by using dark beads. As with all drop styles, remember to consider the weight when choosing stones.

REQUIREMENTS
Two oval crystal beads 1.6 cm (⁹⁄₁₆ in) long
Four oval crystal beads 1.4 cm (½ in) long
Two dark red drop beads 1.7 cm (⅝ in) long
Two gold triple loop links
Four gold beads 4 mm (²⁄₁₀ in) diameter
Four gold beads 3 mm (⅛ in) diameter
Two small size gold bellcaps with claws
*Two eyepins 3 cm (1⅛ in) long, or make
    them from two 4 cm (1⁶⁄₁₀ in) lengths of
    0.8 mm (0.03 in) wire*
Four gold headpins 2.6 cm (1 in) long
Two 5 mm (³⁄₁₆ in) jump rings

Making the earrings:
1 On to an eyepin pass first one of the larger gold beads, followed by a larger crystal bead and another larger gold bead. Loop the eyepin at both ends.

2 To one end of the eyepin attach an earring fitting, and attach the other end of

the eyepin to the single loop side of a triple loop link, checking that any pattern on this is facing outwards, to correspond with the position of the ear fitting.

3 Take two headpins and to each add first a small gold bead followed by one of the smaller crystal beads. Loop the end of each headpin through an outer loop on the triple loop link.

Sparkling cut crystal and plastic 'jewels' come shaped as drops, or with flat backs. They make marvellous party earrings.

4 Glue a bellcap to a dark red drop bead. When dry, use a jump ring to attach it to the center loop on the triple loop link. Repeat for the other earring.

Variations:
Large plastic 'crystal' drops are light to wear, and silver fittings complement their coloring. Thread small black beads and a larger, crystal bead on to an eyepin, and link it to a bellcap and glued-in drop. A large domed earring clip balances the design well.

Green gems and crystals create dramatic party earrings. As none of the flat-backed paste stones used in the design have drilled holes, they are glued (at the top) to flat disc clip fittings with an integral loop, and for the drop, to a fancy shaped drilled backplate.

Wooden curtain ring earrings

Curtain hoops can be adapted for earring hoops, as despite their spectacular size, they are very light to wear. You can hide their origins in a variety of ways by painting or wrapping the base wood. If you are making large hoop earrings, you could also consider making a matching necklace or a linked belt from smaller rings.

REQUIREMENTS
Wooden curtain hoops in a variety of sizes and finishes
Earring fittings: domed, flat disc, with and without loops
Enamel paints, craft brushes and varnish
Lengths of bright or metallic ribbon
Wire in gold and silver
Small ribbon bows
Sewing machine bobbins
Instant bonding glue
Epoxy resin glue
Pliers, wire cutters, hand drill with a 0.8 mm (0.03 in) drill bit

Binding hoops with ribbon:
The best results are achieved with narrow ribbon or braid, as this fits the curve of the curtain ring closely. A large hoop will require about 50 cm (20 in) ribbon. Remove any screw curtain hook fitting, and start binding by securing the end of the ribbon to the hoop with instant bonding glue.

Angle the ribbon slightly, to follow the binding direction and, overlapping the ribbon edges slightly, wind the ribbon round as tightly as possible, to prevent it from slipping, until it overlaps the starting end. Trim the ribbon and glue the end to what will become the back of the hoop.

Attaching earring fittings:

The simplest way to do this is to use the drilled hole left from the curtain hook, and to make a peg and loop shape from 1.2 mm (0.05 in) wire to fit into this hole. Stick the peg in place with epoxy resin glue. You can then add an earring fitting to this loop.

Twisted wire loops:

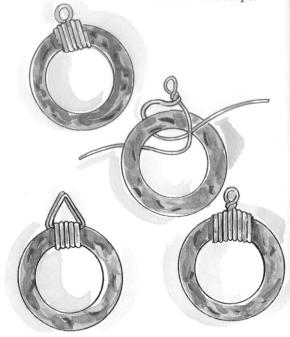

An alternative way to add a fitting is to wind a coil of wire round the decorated hoop, at what will become the top of the earring. You can attach a separate loop to this wire coil, or you can twist the wire itself into a loop to hold a fitting.

To make an integral loop, twist the middle of a length of wire into a loop, then sit this loop on top of the wooden hoop. Wind the remaining wire in opposite directions round the hoop. There should be enough tension in the wire to hold it tightly in place without glue.

Alternatively, wind the wire round the hoop three, four or five times and then, taking a thinner wire, pass it through the coil on top of the hoop. Pass it through again to form a double loop and cut off any excess wire. File to smooth end if necessary.

> **Note:** *Many of the fastenings and decorative ideas used for these wooden earrings could be adapted to transform shiny metal and plastic hoops.*

Opposite: *Different effects on simple wooden curtain rings: a sponged paint finish, wrapping with tartan ribbon and 'friendly plastic' and with silver wire.*

'Friendly plastic' wrapped hoops

Wrap this fascinating new material round small curtain hoops, then hang them from eye-catching studs made from a sewing machine bobbin!

REQUIREMENTS
Two wooden hoops 4 cm (1⁹/₁₆ in) diameter
Green 'friendly plastic'; one 17.7 cm (6¹⁵/₁₆ in) strip, or more if applying it thickly
One chrome or silver sewing machine bobbin
Silver wire 1.0 mm diameter, two 12 cm (4⁵/₈ in) lengths
Two silver jump rings
Two flat earring fittings
Instant bonding glue
Round nosed pliers, file and wire cutters
Small pan of hot water, plastic spatula

Covering the hoops with 'friendly plastic':

1 Cut the plastic into strips about 1 cm (³/₈ in) wide. It is practical to work with about six strips at one time.
2 Place the strips in the pan of hot – not boiling – water. The strips will become pliable very quickly. Lift them out one at a time with the spatula and immediately fold the strips to cover the whole of each hoop. If the plastic hardens too quickly, immerse the hoops in water to re-soften the plastic.

3 Push the pliable plastic very gently round each hoop, to avoid spoiling the surface sheen. Careful shaping will help reveal a little of the reverse color – in this case blue. Continue until the hoops are completely covered, and leave to dry.

Making the earrings:

1 Make a twisted wire loop on the top of each hoop. Take a sewing machine bobbin and, using pliers, discard the central barrel.

2 Cut pieces of 'friendly plastic' from the strip, sufficient to cover the back of each bobbin end. Soften the plastic in hot water then, with the green side facing downwards, push each plastic piece into the back of a bobbin end, pressing well into the drilled holes. Trim the edge to shape.
3 While the plastic is still slightly soft, push a sharp point through the plastic in one of the drilled holes, to make a hole for a link. Twist a file in the hole to make it neater on the green side.

4 You may need to use glue to make the plastic stick to the back of the bobbin end. Glue an earring fitting to the back of the plastic, then pass a jump ring through the pierced hole in the bobbin. Link this to the loop on the hoop.

Variations:

Large, sponge-painted hoops become drops by hanging them from flat-backed domed studs with chunky wire and jump rings.

Wire-bound wooden hoops are simple and effective. Paint the hoops gold, then coil copper wire followed by silver wire, round the lower parts of the hoop. Secure the ends with instant bonding glue.

Tartan wrapped earrings with bows can be made to complement an outfit. For each wrapped earring make a twisted wire loop, then thread a short eyepin through a tiny bow and attach one end of the pin to the loop and the other end to an ear fitting.

Pierced metal shapes as earrings

Cutting shapes from small pieces of sheet metal will open up all kinds of design possibilities to you. Initially you may find that the inevitable broken saw blades are a frustration, but it is well worth persevering to develop the skill. Begin by cutting one of the more simple shapes shown here.

If you are not able to obtain small pieces of metal sheet you will find that most craft shops sell inexpensive copper shapes for enamelling. These are useful as you can pierce small shapes from larger shapes.

Once you feel able to produce well finished pieces, you may wish to use real silver sheet. This is available from precious metal dealers. Sheet of 1.0 mm (0.04 in) thickness is sufficient for most designs.

(See the **How to begin** chapter pages 12 to 23 for information on tools and materials, and page 14 for how to transfer a design to metal and use a piercing saw.)

These 'man in the moon' and star earrings are designs worked in copper with a piercing saw. As this is a soft, easy to work metal, it is ideal for this technique.

Riveting:

If you would like to use a contrasting backplate, perhaps wood, plastic or another color of metal, you can simply glue the pierced shape to the backplate with epoxy resin. However, for a more secure join, you can rivet the front to the back. Ideally, the rivets should be both decorative and functional, as shown in the following carring designs.

To rivet pieces together, first drill holes in the top, pierced shape at the points where you consider a rivet would add strength.

Making rivets:

Place the pierced shape over the backplate (it may help to glue the two shapes together to hold them firm), and drill carefully straight through the holes into the backplate, until you have drilled right through the backplate.

Next select a wire that fits tightly into the drilled holes. (If you use a 1.0 mm (0.04 in) drill bit, use a 1.0 mm wire rivet.) If the drill bit has moved slightly during drilling the wire may be a little loose. In this case, use a thicker wire for the rivet and file it down until it fits tightly in the hole.

Cut the wire so that it protrudes a little above the front and back surfaces by about 0.5 mm, ready for hammering flat.

On flat metal surfaces you can hammer the rivet with the flat face of a hammer. Do this first on one side, then turn the piece over and hammer on the other side. The aim is to spread the ends of the wire rivet so that the two plates are held together.

On a wooden or plastic surface work in the same way, but protect the surface with a cloth under the hammer, to prevent the surface from marking. Always hammer lightly to avoid splitting the material.

Countersinking rivets:

To create a more professional finish you can countersink the rivets by filing inside the holes with a round file. Then, when the rivet is hammered, it can be filed flush.

Polishing and finishing:
After riveting, polish the piece carefully with fine sandpaper, followed by Tripoli and rouge. To make stud earrings, glue the stud to the back of the piece, or for drop styles, drill a hole near the top of the earring.

Star earrings
These are an easy shape to start with, and you do not need to be too accurate – irregular edges will make the design look like starfish. The surface texture is created by hammering a nail into the metal.

REQUIREMENTS
*Two copper shapes 4.5 cm (1¾ in) diameter
    and 1.0 mm (0.04 in) thickness
Jewelers' piercing saw
Sawblades size 2/0
Flat file
Masonry nail
General use ball-peen hammer
Drill and 1.5 mm (0.06 in) drill bit
Tripoli and rouge polish
Copper wire 1.2 mm (0.05 in) diameter,
    about 4 cm (1½ in) long (to make 10
    jump rings)*

*Two flat plate earring fittings
Epoxy resin adhesive
Tracing paper
Clear enamel varnish*

Making the earrings:
1 Trace the star shape and transfer it to the metal, either by re-drawing it on the metal or by gluing the tracing directly to the surface with stick adhesive.
2 Saw out the shape with a piercing saw, and file round the edges to make the shape more regular, if this is necessary.
3 Working on a hard surface, mark a textured pattern into the metal by hammering the masonry nail at random over one side of the shape. The star may become distorted, in which case gently hammer the reverse side to flatten. Drill a hole near the tip of one of the points.

4 Using the picture as a guide, make triangular ear studs from a copper remnant. Drill the studs near the tips of the triangles. File round the edges and hammer the texture as before.

5 If the hammering has created raised bumps on the reverse side of the shapes, use this as the front of the design. If not, the indented nail marks will still look attractive, and you can use these as the right side. Join the shapes together with jump rings made from the copper wire (five for each earring).

6 Glue the earring fitting to the back of the top triangle. To avoid the copper tarnishing, varnish over the whole design with a coat of clear varnish.

'Man in the moon' earrings

Although this is a more complex design, it is a good exercise once you have gained confidence with a piercing saw. To follow the lines with a sawblade, take your time and avoid pushing forward. Maneuver the piece gently to get the cut moving in the right direction.

REQUIREMENTS
Two copper discs 3.5 cm (1⁵/₁₆ in) diameter and 1.0 mm (0.04 in) thick
Two wooden discs 3.5 cm (1⁵/₁₆ in) diameter and 2.5 mm (³/₃₂ in) thick
Piercing saw and size 2/0 sawblades
Hand drill and 1.0 (0.04 in) mm drill bit
Copper wire 1.0 mm (0.04 in) diameter, 8 cm (3¹/₈ in) long
Two flat plate earring fittings
Ball-peen hammer
Flat file
Tripoli and rouge polish and polishing sticks
Instant bonding glue
Tracing paper

Practice cutting out shapes with a piercing saw so that you gain confidence with the technique. Glue the shapes to a background material, then drill through both layers. Make rivets to fit the holes tightly.

Making the earrings:
1 Trace the 'man in the moon' shape and transfer it to the metal disc. Slowly cut out the shape, then file round the edges to neaten the shape.

2 Glue the moon shape to the wooden disc. Drill holes through the metal and wooden backplate at the top and base of the moon. Also drill three holes in the wood to the side of the moon shape for rivet 'stars'.

3 Cut copper wire to fit each hole tightly, and so it protrudes slightly. With the work resting securely on a flat metal surface, hammer the rivets gently from both sides until the wire ends spread slightly.

4 If the metal surface becomes scratched, rub the area with fine sandpaper, then rub with Tripoli and rouge polishes.

5 Glue earring fittings to the wooden backplates, near to the top. Varnish the whole piece if you wish, to prevent tarnishing.

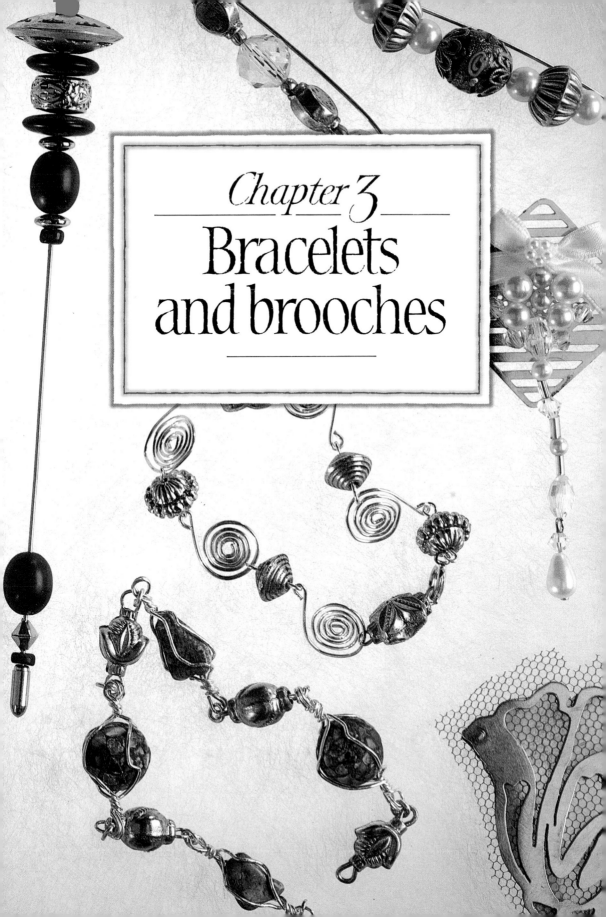

Chapter 3
Bracelets
and brooches

Bracelets, bangles and brooches are pieces of jewelry where individual tastes seem to vary most. They are often a very bold statement of personal style, and are generally worn to be noticed.

The designs in this chapter represent a broad cross section of styles, and are made from a variety of materials; some of these are familiar, while others are not.

Brooch backs are available in various styles and sizes. Hatpins can also be made into bar brooches by twisting the long wire stem to shape.

In most cases, simply gluing a brooch fitting to the back of the design is satisfactory. For heavy or large brooches, glue the fitting quite high up on the back to avoid the brooch falling forward.

Brass cord holders with drops

These oval brass shapes are used to hold cord at the end of window blinds, but their shiny, reflective quality gives them potential for jewelry making. Besides making them into bracelets you could link them together to make a chunky chain belt.

REQUIREMENTS
Five domed brass cord holders
Nine oval links from brass chain
Ten gold bead cups
Five oval beads 1.2 cm (½ in) long
Five gold headpins
Jump rings and a bolt ring
Pliers and wire cutters

Making the bracelet:

1 Start by beading the headpins. Add to the headpin one bead cup, a bead and another bead cup. Bend the top of the headpin into a loop and cut off any excess wire.

Cord holders, joined with brass links make up this bracelet. The ceramic bead drops are suspended from matching brass links.

2 Cut the brass links open with wire cutters, cutting at the center of one of the long sides. Join the brass cord holders together with the links. Open up the links and slip them through the holes at the sides of the holders, making sure they are all facing the same way. Close the links tightly with pliers.

3 Fit a link to the hole in the dome of the center cord holder, and attach a beaded headpin. Add the remaining beaded headpins in the same way. Complete the bracelet by attaching jump rings to each end, and a bolt ring fitting.

Twisted wire links bracelet

Decorative wire links used between beads can create different effects. Designs can vary from delicate pieces created with fine wire and small, intricate beads, through to bold, dramatic bracelets formed with thicker wire and large, colorful beads.

REQUIREMENTS
Silver wire 0.8 mm (0.03 in) diameter
Six silver decorative beads 1.5 cm (⅝ in)
  long, three different pairs
Silver bracelet fastening
Round nosed pliers and wire cutters

Making the bracelet:

1   Cut a 13 cm (5¹/₁₆ in) length of 0.8 mm wire. Using the pliers, twist this into a closely coiled flat disc. Leave the last 2 cm (¾ in) straight and bend the very end of this into a loop. Twist it in the opposite direction from the coil. Make five coils.
2   Cut wire to make looped pins for the beads. Thread the wire through the bead and leave an extra 1 cm (⅜ in) at each side. Twist this extra into a loop at each side, so that the loop sits firmly against the side of the bead.

3   Link the beads to the flat coiled units. You will have to open the loop on the straight part of the coil to slide on a bead. Slide the first bead right round to the outside of the coil. Attach another bead to the open loop on the coil, and close it.
4   Continue to link the bracelet together, making sure that all the flat coiled discs are laying the same way. Attach the bracelet fastenings to the end loops on the beads.

Variations:
Use copper or brass wire with silvered beads or bright ceramic beads. Try making tubular coiled wire units between beads, or coils of different colored metals linked together.

Delicate silver scroll links contrast well with the more solid looking silver beads in this bracelet design.

Wire wrapped beads

This is a really good way to display natural, undrilled stones, as well as beads. The simple, effective technique offers lots of scope for improvisation.

REQUIREMENTS
Beads and stones
Gold, silver or copper wire 0.8 mm (0.03 in)
*   diameter*
Bracelet fastenings
Round nosed pliers and wire cutters

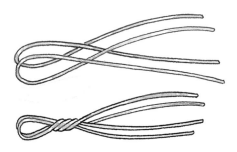

Wrapping beads in wire 'cages':
There are various ways to wrap wire round beads and stones; this method is very easy. Take a length of 0.8 mm wire, and fold it in half loosely. You will require about 18 cm (7 in) for a 2.5 cm (1 in) diameter bead. Cut another wire length the same, and fold this in half. Holding the wires together, twist a loop in the center. This creates a secure

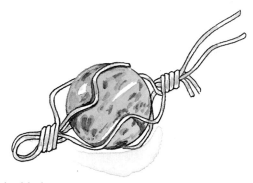

double loop with four wires.
Place the bead or stone inside this wire 'cage'. At the other end, wind two of the loose wires round to form a loop. Wind the other two round the base of the loop.
Next, use the pliers to twist the wires over the bead or stone, so that the wires follow its shape.

Wired turquoise and silver bead bracelet
A mixture of turquoise beads and rough turquoise chips are linked to smaller, decorative silver beads.
The result is a beautifully balanced, modern design.

REQUIREMENTS
Two turquoise beads 1.5 cm (⅝ in) diameter
Two smaller, rough turquoise chips
Three silver beads 1.2 cm (½ in) diameter
Silver wire 0.8 mm (0.03 in) diameter
Silver bolt ring fastening and jump ring

Making the bracelet:
1 Wire-wrap the turquoise beads and chips. Make sure the wires are evenly placed around the shapes.
2 Pass a length of silver wire through each of the silver beads, and bend this into a loop at each side. Before closing the loops

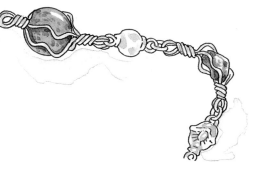

completely, attach the wire wrapped beads.
3 To do this, start with a turquoise bead, followed by a silver bead, then a turquoise chip, then a silver bead. Continue in this way until the last turquoise chip. Close the loops securely as you link the beads. Do this by twisting the wire tightly around itself, or by pushing it back into the silver bead.
4 To finish the bracelet, attach a jump ring to the loop at the end of the last silver bead, and a bolt ring to the turquoise chip at the other end of the bracelet.

Variations:
Colored glass marbles could be used in the cages instead of beads. Look for striking designs in clear or opaque glass.

Coordinate large wire wrapped beads with smaller beads of the same design, by linking them between the cages.

Note: Experiment with different effects by making the cages from a mixture of colored metals: try combining copper and silver together, or gold and silver wire.

Simple rough-cut stones like turquoise and amber are a perfect choice for wire cage designs. The effect is complemented by the introduction of contrasting beads, as with the silver beads used between the cages in this design.

Fabric-wrapped bangles

You can transform inexpensive plastic bangles in a matter of minutes by covering them with ribbons or 'friendly plastic'.

Bead trims, braids and sequins can also be used to add contrast to the background fabric. You could also add coins or charms.

REQUIREMENTS
Flat or curved bangles with a smooth
*   surface*
Wired-edge ribbon
Ribbons or tapes
'Friendly plastic'
Instant bonding glue

Wrapping bangles with ribbon:
Use ribbons that are 2 cm (¾ in) wide or less for wrapping the bangles, as wider ribbons will not wrap so evenly.

The length of ribbon required will depend on the width of the bangle and the ribbon; wind a tape round to make a rough estimate, then allow a little extra for neatening ends.

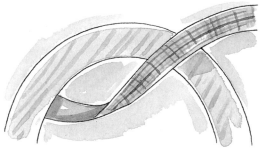

Glue the ribbon end diagonally to the inside of the bangle, then wrap the ribbon round and round the bangle. Wrap the ribbon tightly, keeping an even tension throughout, and overlapping the ribbon sides by about 5 mm (³⁄₁₆ in). If the fabric is particularly heavy it is helpful to spread a little glue over the entire bangle before wrapping the fabric.

When the bangle is completely wrapped, trim the ribbon end and tuck it out of sight inside the bangle. Secure with glue.

Metallic ribbon-wrapped bangles
These two bangles are designed to be worn together. Both are wrapped with co-ordinating metallic weave ribbon and wrapped again with a narrow gold ribbon.

REQUIREMENTS
Two plastic bangles 1 cm (⅜ in) wide
Two 65 cm (25½ in) lengths of check ribbon
*   2 cm (¾ in) wide*
Two 50 cm (19½ in) lengths of gold ribbon
*   5 mm (³⁄₁₆ in) wide*
Instant bonding glue

Making the bangles:
1 Wrap each bangle with the check ribbon and secure the ends.

2 Starting at the same point as for the check ribbon, glue and wrap the gold ribbon over the check wrappings. Position the ribbon so that there is about 1.5 cm (⁹⁄₁₆ in) between each rotation. Aim to wind the ribbon so that it ends at the starting point. Glue the end to the inside of the bangle.

Variations:
'Friendly plastic' can be cut into strips and wrapped ribbon-style round a bangle. Heat the strips a few at a time, and mold each one into place. Fill in the gaps with more strips. The end result will look like leather or metal, depending on the chosen pattern.

Ruched ribbon bangle
Wired-edge ribbon is ideal for creating 'instant' party bangles. It is used extensively in floral art and display work and is available from craft shops and florists' suppliers in deep, rich colors and metallic finishes. Try using two colors together.

REQUIREMENTS
One plastic bangle 1 cm (⅜ in) wide
One 75 cm (30 in) length of metallic wired-
*   edge ribbon 5 cm (2 in) wide*
Needle and invisible thread

Making the bangle:
1 Slip the ribbon over the bangle with both wired edges level. Use running stitch to hold the ribbon in place, along the outer curve of the bangle.

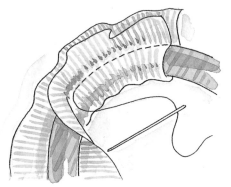

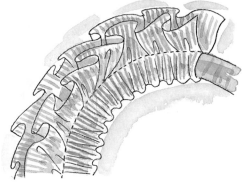

2 As you sew, gather the ribbon as you work, until the entire length of ribbon is taken up. Overlap the ends slightly, work a few backstitches to secure, then ruffle the ribbon edges to shape.

Metallic trimmed ribbons, and wired-edged ribbons can quickly 'dress up' plain bangles, so you can design them to match a special outfit. 'Friendly plastic' is another versatile material which offers the same options.

Hat pins with ornate beads

As hats can transform the wearer, so hat pins can transform a hat – or at least complement it perfectly. Even if you do not wear a hat regularly, you can still make use of a hat pin, by wearing it in the lapel of a jacket, or as a striking scarf pin.

Black and gold beaded hat pin

This design has an Oriental quality, suggested by the pierced brass bead and the black washers. You can vary the effect by retaining the last three beads to use as a decorative touch for the end of the pin. Simply slide them in place before fastening the hat pin.

   If you cannot copy the design closely, use the shape and color of the beads as a guide to create your own designs.

REQUIREMENTS
One gold lapel/hat pin 15.5 cm (6³/₃₂ in) long and a pin protector
One pierced brass disc bead 2.7 cm (1¹/₁₆ in) diameter
Two black washers 1.7 cm (1¹¹/₁₆ in) diameter
Flat gold bead 1.3 cm (½ in) diameter
Two gold washers 8.0 mm (⁵/₁₆ in) diameter
Two oval black beads 14 mm (⁹/₁₆ in) long
Three black rocaille beads 5 mm (³/₁₆ in) diameter
One gold bead 7 mm (¼ in) long
Instant bonding glue (or a French crimp)

Making the hat pin:
1 First pass on one of the black rocaille beads. This should fit the pin very tightly. If not, glue it in place at the end of the pin.

2 Next pass on the flat, pierced brass disc, a black washer, the flat gold bead, a black washer, a small gold washer, an oval black bead, a small gold washer, a rocaille bead.

The hat pins here make good use of ornate metal disc beads, as their shapes contrast well with the other simple bead shapes.

(Glue this last bead in place if you wish to add the remaining pins to the end of the hat pin, or add a French crimp.)

3 Continue with an oval black bead, the gold bead and a rocaille bead. Glue this last bead in place, or add a French crimp.

Variations:
Bronze, brass and copper beads look equally effective, and would blend well with many background colors. The large copper disc bead dominates the design.

Bar brooches from hat pins

Make these by bending the end of a hat pin into a hook, and threading half the pin with beads. The remainder of the pin is bent over to form the fastening bar. Many types of beads can be used to decorate the pin, but they should be small enough not to cause the pin to arch when threaded.

REQUIREMENTS
Hat pins
Beads, not more than 15 mm (⁹⁄₁₆ in) diameter
Small washer beads (to fit the pin tightly)
Round nosed pliers
A flat file

Making a lapel pin:

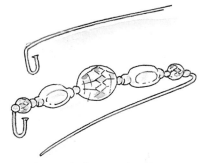

Use round nosed pliers to bend 1 cm (³⁄₈ in) downwards at the end of a pin. Pass on a small washer bead followed by your chosen bead sequence; cover just under half the length of the pin, ending with another washer bead. Make sure you do not have too many beads, as the pin will not reach the hook when twisted to shape.

Use pliers to bend the pin close to the last washer bead. Bend it underneath the beads so that the point of the pin sits into the twisted hook. Make sure the beaded part of the pin is not too arched, and that the pin end sits neatly into the hook. If the pin is too long, cut off the excess and use a flat file to re-shape the end to a point.

Silver and crystal lapel pin
REQUIREMENTS
A silver hat pin 12 cm (4⁶⁄₈ in) long
One 13 mm (⁹⁄₁₆ in) diameter cut crystal bead
Two 7 mm (¼ in) diameter crystal beads
Two flat silver beads 12 mm (½ in) long
Six silver beads 3 mm (⅛ in) diameter

Making the brooch:
1 Bend the pin end to shape, and thread the beads in the following order: a small silver bead, one of the smaller crystal beads, a small silver bead, a flat silver bead, a small silver bead, the large crystal bead, a small silver bead, a flat silver bead, a small silver bead, a small crystal bead, a small silver bead.
2 Bend the remaining unbeaded pin behind the beads, making sure that the end fits into the hook. Adjust as necessary.

Variations
A decorative Venetian glass bead trimmed with bead cups works well at the center of a bar brooch. Two large, grooved gold beads balance the shape, and contrast well with the smaller pearl beads.

These attractive bar brooches made from bent hat pins belie their humble origins.

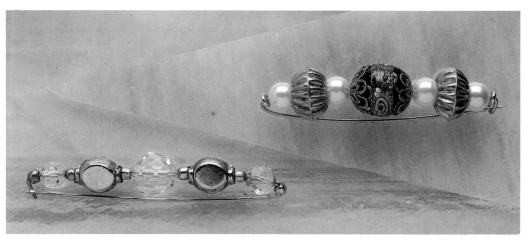

Pierced metal brooches

The piercing saw technique is covered in the **How to begin** chapter, and is used to make the rivetted earrings in the **Earrings** chapter. Look at the information there if you have not used these techniques before.

Floral brooch with netting

This large floral shape is pierced from silver colored metal, with a brass backplate. You could substitute aluminium or copper for the brooch for a different effect.

REQUIREMENTS
Piece of gauge 8 (gauge 25 U.S.A.) silver sheet metal, about 10 cm (4 in) square
Piece of 8 gauge brass sheet, about 10 cm (4 in) square
Piercing saw and size 0/2 sawblades
Drill and 1 mm (0.04 in) drill bit
1 mm (0.04 in) wire
A ball-peen hammer
Tracing paper, pencil, scissors
Bright pink net fabric, larger than metal sheet
A brooch pin
Instant bonding glue
*(See the **How to begin** chapter page 14 for how to transfer designs for piercing.)*

Pierced and rivetted metal shapes can look good mounted over wood or fabric.

Making the brooch:

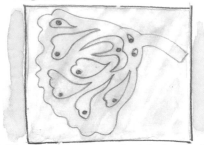

1 Trace the design, and stick the tracing on to the silver metal. Drill holes in the areas to be cut out. Put the saw blade into these holes carefully, then slowly cut out the waste areas.
2 Continue by cutting out the whole shape from the sheet by cutting round the outline. Use the same method to cut around the outline of the back plate.
3 Mark the position for three rivets on the top silver plate, and drill holes. Place this over the backplate and mark the corresponding positions through the holes with the tip of the drill bit.
4 Remove the silver plate and drill holes in the backplate.
5 Hand polish the shapes thoroughly.
6 Spread a little glue on the underside of the pierced silver plate, and press the net to this. Then position the back plate underneath. Squeeze the layers together.
7 Push wire through the rivet holes, and cut and file the rivets close to the surface at the back and front. Hammer them flat, turning from front to back to ensure the wire ends spread evenly at both sides.

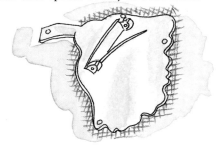

8 Glue the brooch pin to the upper part of the backplate, and trim the netting. Leave a little all round the edge for interest.

Variations:

Pierce an abstract shape in copper, polish it, then rivet it to a dark wood backplate. Glue the brooch fitting to the back of the wood.

Pierced screen beaded brooch

Differently shaped metal screens with pierced holes are available for making beaded brooches. Once beaded, the screen clips over a pinned backplate. More unusual however, are the brooch backs like the one shown here, that are designed for cross stitch embroidery. These flat, geometric shapes have panels for the stitching, but these can also be used for beaded designs.

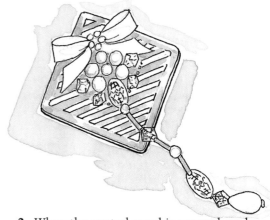

REQUIREMENTS

*One gold diamond shaped cross stitch
    brooch fitting with a smaller central
    diamond panel of small holes
A small ivory colored ribbon bow, trimmed
    with tiny pearls
Two pearls 7 mm (⁵/₁₆ in) diameter
Three pearls 6 mm (⁷/₃₂ in) diameter
Three pearls 5 mm (³/₁₆ in) diameter
One teardrop pearl 1 cm (³/₈ in) long
Six crystal beads 5 mm (³/₁₆ in) long
Two oval crystal beads 1 cm (³/₈ in) long
Three gold tube beads
One small gold headpin
Nylon gut, threading needle and pin
Instant bonding glue*

Making the brooch:

1 Begin by sewing the small bow to the top of the central pierced panel with nylon gut. From this point take the needle through to the front of the brooch. Pass on one of the 5 mm (³/₁₆ in) pearls and take the gut through another hole to the back of the brooch. Using the picture as a guide, continue sewing on the beads by passing the gut from the front to the back of the brooch. Arrange one oval crystal centrally at the base of the center panel, and the smaller crystals round the edge of the pearls.

2 When the central panel is covered, make the drop. To do this, take the gut through to the front of the lowest point of the panel and thread on a pearl, a gold tube, a crystal, a gold tube, a pearl, a gold tube, an oval crystal. Leave a loop at the end of this final crystal, and hold it in place with a pin. Pass the gut back up through the hanging beads and up to the back of the brooch. Stitch or tie the gut, and secure with a drop of glue.

3 To add the final drop pearl and crystal, add them to the headpin. Bend the end of the pin into a loop, and cut off any excess. Attach this headpin to the loop of gut protruding from the oval crystal.

Pearl and crystal beads, and a bow trim contrast well with the gold brooch backing.

Painted silk brooches

Attractive brooch frames are now available from craft shops, and these are ideal for mounting scraps of painted silk. You do not have to be 'an artist' to achieve something pretty; just paint some colorful abstract shapes. This style of brooch is very quick to make too – you can paint a design to complement a scarf or outfit.

Use special silk paints which become fixed by ironing over them, or simply paint a design with colored inks or fabric pens.

REQUIREMENTS
A brooch frame with glass, about 6 cm
  (2⅜ in) long
A piece of card to fit inside the brooch
  frame
A scrap of ivory silk or satin to fit over the
  card insert
Silk paints or colored inks
A black drawing pen and pencil
A fine watercolor paint brush
A sheet of scrap paper
Craft glue and scissors

Making the brooch:
1   Draw lightly round the brooch backplate on to card and cut out. Trim to fit inside the frame. Draw round the card on to silk to outline the design area, and lay the silk on to scrap paper to protect the work surface.

Mount a tiny scrap of painted silk in a frame, and it comes alive with color. This painted design has been overlaid with silver mesh.

Draw a design – some abstract flower shapes for example – with the pen. Dip the paintbrush lightly in the first color ink and apply it with light touches so the ink runs into the fibers.
2   Add more colors in this way to fill in the outlines, then apply some lighter color to create background shapes. Leave to dry, then cut out the silk 3 mm (⅛ in) outside the drawn outline.

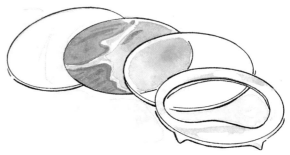

3   Dab a little glue along the edges of the card shape and press the fabric over this. Apply more glue to the wrong side of the card to secure the overlapping fabric. When this is dry, assemble the brooch parts.

'Friendly plastic' brooches

You can make interesting designs simply by twisting and folding this material to shape. Collect different colors and finishes and save scraps left from other projects, as these can all be incorporated into designs for brooches or, with different fastenings, into hairclips, tie-tacks or cuff links.

The pieces here were made by softening the plastic in an oven and in warm water.

(See the **How to Begin** chapter page 20 for more information on 'friendly plastic')

Folded brooch with diamanté stones

REQUIREMENTS
Half a long strip of pearlized 'friendly plastic'
Three small pieces of gold 'friendly plastic', each about 1 cm (⅜ in) square
Three diamanté stones 8 mm (¼ in) diameter
Sequin waste
A baking tray lined with oiled foil
An oven at 100 °c (212 °f)
A bowl of warm water
Sharp scissors
Brooch back
Epoxy resin glue

Making the brooch:
1 Begin by softening the plastic in warm water. Press the sequin waste into the surface. Remove this when the plastic has cooled, and you will see a pattern of circles.

2 Cut the embossed plastic in half and overlap each piece on the baking tray. Heat in the oven until the plastic is pliable, then remove the tray, and crease the foil under the plastic into folds so that the plastic follows the contours.
3 While this is cooling, place the three diamanté stones on top of the gold squares. Warm these on foil in the oven until the plastic is soft, and press the stones down into the plastic. When cool, trim the plastic round the edges of the stones.

4 Glue the diamanté stones in position on the gold plastic shapes, then glue these in a row down the overlapping center of the folded embossed section.
5 Finally, glue a brooch fastening to the back of the brooch.

Variations:
Cut long multi-colored strips of plastic, and arrange them in a flame-like design on foil. Bake in the oven, before gluing to a hairclip or brooch fastening.

Overlay contrasting scraps of plastic at right angles to give an appearance of continuous folds and swirling patterns. Cut sufficient to cover a large hair ornament, then bake the arrangement in the oven. Shape the warm plastic over the hairclip, and glue it in place.

'Friendly plastic' offers lots of scope for design ideas. By pressing sequins into the surface create texture, or arrange colored scraps at random.

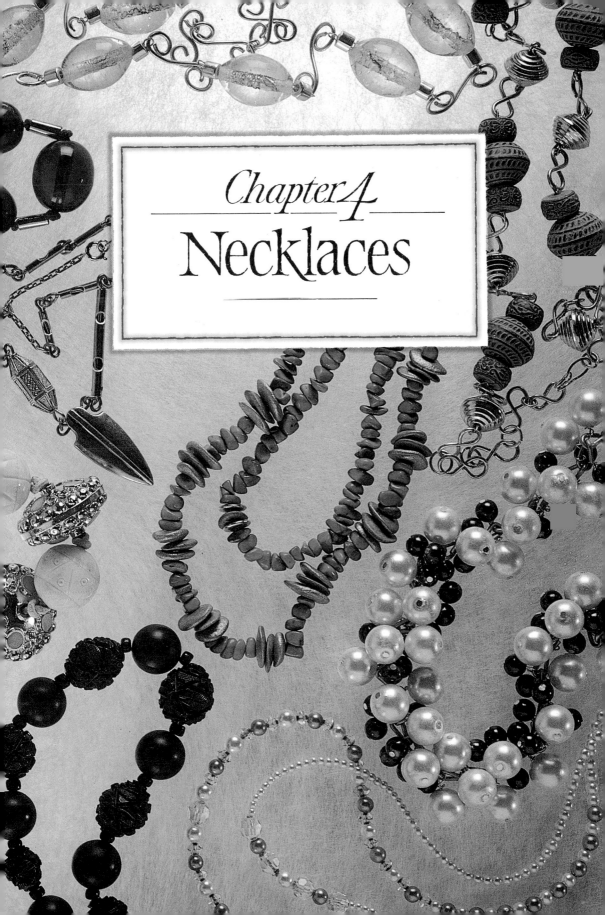

Chapter 4
Necklaces

A 'necklace' can describe anything from a single wire choker to long, multiple strands of tiny seed beads or ropes of boldly patterned ceramic and glass beads; the variety of styles is enormous and gives plenty of scope for creative designs.

Everyone has their own idea of what suits them or their personality so, with this in mind, the necklace designs in this chapter are samples of quite diverse styles. As with most of the designs in this book, a different color scheme will alter the finished effect.

Many of the designs can be worked with materials you already have around you, or with things that you can obtain easily. All the projects are simple to make once you have the basic materials.

Necklaces from broken beads

This project should give you ideas on how to transform broken necklaces and strings of beads. By re-stringing the beads you can also change necklaces that are never worn because they are the 'wrong' color, or have some unattractive elements.

Changing the color sequence, adding new beads – perhaps mixing patterned beads with plain – will completely alter the appearance of a necklace. Fancy clasps and plain or ornate bead cups are available in gold and silver finishes, and these are very useful for 'dressing' plain beads, to give them a more expensive, sophisticated look.

REQUIREMENTS
Broken necklace beads
Nylon gut for threading, silk, or waxed
    polyester thread, a bead threader
Necklace fastenings: calotte crimps with
    bolt rings, screw fastenings or hook and
    eye fastenings
Chain nosed pliers and tweezers
Instant bonding glue
*(See the **How to begin** chapter page 21 for*
    details on threading and knotting.)

Beads from broken necklaces offer a marvellous choice for creating new designs. You can incorporate beads from several necklaces to create totally different looks, and transform unexciting plain beads by trimming them with ornate bead caps.

Threading beads:

This is done most easily with nylon gut, as this thread passes through beads easily without a needle. Because it is strong it is also a practical choice for threading heavier beads. Beads with a very narrow drilled hole may need silk or polyester thread.

Sorting beads:

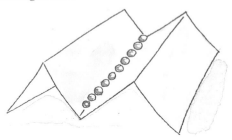

To re-arrange beads ready for stringing, fold a sheet of paper concertina-fashion, and lay the beads in the center fold. This will keep them in order, and help you to sort out small beads and color and size sequences.

Necklace fastenings:

Any type of necklace fastening can be used. You may be able to re-use the original clasp, perhaps with a calotte crimp. A calotte crimp will give a neat, professional appearance at the end of the thread, as the knot is hidden, enclosed in the cup-shaped crimp. Use chain nosed pliers to open the loop on the necklace fastening, and attach this to the loop on the crimp. If both loops are solid, with no opening, use a jump ring to link the two loops together.

Fitting hollow screw fastenings:

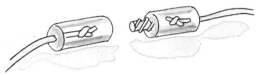

These small, barrel shape fastenings have the thread knots hidden inside each barrel, so a calotte crimp is not needed.

When all the beads on a necklace are threaded, pass the end of the thread into the base end of one half of the hollow screw fastening. Tie a knot and add a touch of instant bonding glue for extra security. Pull the knot back into the hollow barrel. The knot must be big enough to prevent it slipping through the screw fastening when pulled.

To attach the other end of the fastening, thread and secure the barrel in the same way, making sure to tie the knot in the gut as closely as possible to the fastening.

Pearls and crystal rope

This delicate design was made by combining three broken necklaces: a classic but inexpensive cultured pearl necklace with graduating pearls, a string of grey 'synthetic' pearls, and a crystal necklace. The rope is long enough to wear twisted into a double strand, and so there is no need for a clasp.

REQUIREMENTS
Thirty two synthetic grey pearls 8 mm (⁵⁄₁₆ in) diameter
Thirty three cut crystal beads graduating down in size from 10 mm (³⁄₈ in)
One hundred and eighty five cultured pearls graduating in size down from 8 mm (⁵⁄₁₆ in) diameter
Fine nylon gut 110 cm (43 in) for threading

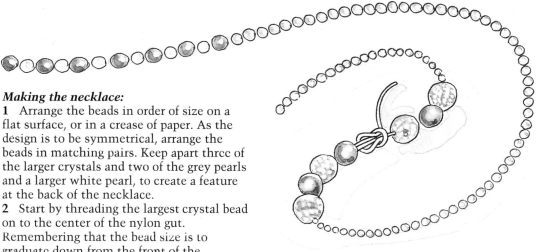

Making the necklace:

1 Arrange the beads in order of size on a flat surface, or in a crease of paper. As the design is to be symmetrical, arrange the beads in matching pairs. Keep apart three of the larger crystals and two of the grey pearls and a larger white pearl, to create a feature at the back of the necklace.

2 Start by threading the largest crystal bead on to the center of the nylon gut. Remembering that the bead size is to graduate down from the front of the necklace to the back, take the arranged pairs and thread them in the following order on each side of the center crystal.

3 Add a white pearl, a crystal, a grey pearl, a crystal, a white pearl and so on. When the crystals are all used, continue to alternate the grey and white pearls until the grey pearls are also all used. Continue to thread the white pearls in order of size.

> **Note:** *The colors of pearls vary considerably; some are very white, while others have a yellow or pinkish hue. Combine these as a feature of the design.*

4 When all the pearls are threaded, thread on the reserved grey and crystal beads, starting with a crystal. Add the center back white pearl then tie off the necklace next to this with a reef knot. Cut off any excess nylon. If possible hide the knot by pulling it back inside the center back pearl. Alternatively, neaten the knot by pushing the ends back into the adjoining beads.

Variations:

Brown crystals mixed with toning plastic beads, gold washers and tiny amber glass beads make up this simple rope necklace.

Gold bead caps enhance the center three black patterned beads, set on a string made up from alternating black and gold beads.

Double strings of beads can be made from one necklace by re-threading the beads with toning tubular beads. Here, iridescent beads match exactly with the inner string of smaller beads.

Antique carved jet from a damaged necklace is given a new lease of life combined with modern plain black beads. An old necklace clasp helps the design retain a convincing period look.

Turquoise chip beads combine well with flat, washer beads. Here some of the turquoise washers are painted a complementary gold.

Gold discs contrast well with turquoise, and toning tubular beads give extra length and added interest to round bead necklaces.

Painted wooden beads on cord

Large wooden beads used for crafts like macramé are ideal for necklaces, as despite their size, they are light to wear.

REQUIREMENTS
Wooden beads in various sizes
Cords in various thicknesses, matching
tassels (optional)
Clear sticky tape and instant bonding glue
Enamel paints and varnish
Artists' paint brushes, toothbrush, synthetic
sponge
*(See the **How to begin** chapter page 20 for*
details on painting or varnishing beads)

Selecting cords and paints:
Cords in different thicknesses and a wide choice of colors are available from notions and furnishing departments. To ensure a good color balance between painted beads and cord it is worth selecting the cord before choosing the shades of paint to go with it.

You can color the beads in lots of different ways; paint techniques like marbling, stippling and sponging need not be reserved for home decorating; you can transform all sizes and shapes of beads with these effects.

To knot beads on cord:
When estimating how much cord is needed for a necklace, remember to allow extra for the knotting. The beads are held in place with a knot at each side, and knots in thick cords will reduce its length quickly.

Before threading beads, first stabilize the ends of the cord by wrapping sticky tape round them to prevent them from fraying.

Thread a bead to the center of the cord, and tie a knot tightly at each side, as close to the bead as possible. Decide on the space between beads, and make another knot at

this point. Add another bead, and knot close to its side as before. Continue in this way, working each side of the central bead to maintain a balance, and shortening or lengthening the space between beads to suit your design.

Cord ties:
As these necklaces are tied loosely at the back of the neck, there is no need for special fastenings. The cord can be left long to hang down as a feature at the back of the necklace, and trimmed with a bead knotted at each end.

Joining thick and thin cords:

You may wish to finish a design with fastening ties in a lighter weight cord. To join thick cord to thinner cord, first pass the thick cord through a bead. Cut a length of thin cord, and prevent the ends from fraying with glue. Make a knot at one end, and push this down inside the bead, next to the thick cord. Take the end of the thick cord and knot this tightly round the thin cord, close to the side of the bead. Wrap sticky tape round the thick cord at the edge of the knot, and cut off the excess through the tape. Secure the ends with glue, and remove the sticky tape.

Stippled wooden bead necklace
This effect is very easy to achieve. By using the paint thickly you can create an attractive raised surface texture. Choose paints to complement the color of the cord.

Simple craft beads, and acorn fittings more usually gracing window blinds, can take on surprising new looks with shiny paint and knotted cord trims, chosen in colors to complement the painted beads.

REQUIREMENTS
One dark wood bead 4 cm (1½ in) diameter
Four dark wood beads 3.5 cm (1⅜ in)
*   diameter*
Two tubular dark wood beads for ends
Enamel paints in orange, green, gold and
*   black, and enamel varnish*
Thick colored cord to match 2 m (78 in)
*   long*
Old toothbrush and mixing dish

Painting the beads:

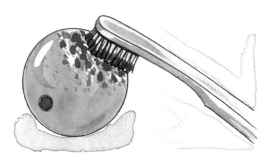

1 Pour a little of the first color paint into
the dish. Dab the toothbrush into this and
tap the beads sharply with color. Paint each
bead with one color at a time to ensure they
are evenly spotted.
2 Allow the paint to touch-dry before
stippling the next color. Clean the
toothbrush between colors, and dry
thoroughly. Continue adding colors until
the beads are evenly stippled, then leave
them to dry. Varnish the beads, and leave
them to dry thoroughly.

Threading the beads:

1 Knot the largest bead at the center of the
cord. Knot on all the stippled beads, keeping
the necklace symmetrical, and leaving gaps
of 4 cm (1½ in) on the cord between knots.
2 Knot the tubular beads on to the ends of
the cords. This cord has been left
deliberately long to allow the beaded ends to
hang down at the back of the neck.

Variations:

Cream marbled beads are threaded next to
gold beads which highlight the subtle shades
of the marbling. Shiny cream cords are
chosen to blend with the beads.

Purple and gold are the predominant colors
in these speckled beads, while green, red and
yellow add subtle glints. All these colors
match the cord and the flecks of metallic
thread that run through it.

Small wooden beads and window blind
'acorn' fittings can be combined to make
unusual bootlace tie necklaces. The cord
ends fit through the 'acorn', which can then
be slipped up and down as desired.

> *Note: Experiment with different types of
> paint. Metal finish paints can create a
> convincing surface on wooden beads.*

*Creamy marble tinged with gold, blends well
with shiny white cord and gold beads.*

Metal tubing on cord or wire

Metal tubing is not always readily available from craft shops, though most jewelry suppliers stock some sizes of gold and silver colored tubing. If you find the diameter is too large for your cord or thong, simply slit the tube at one side and squeeze gently with pliers to reduce the size. Likewise, if the tube is a little too narrow in diameter, slit it and wrap it round the cord.

More expensive silver tubing is available in a wide variety of sizes, including square and triangular shapes. If you do not require a large amount, this is well worth using.

REQUIREMENTS
Beads
Tubing in gold and silver, in different diameters
Cord and chain
Wire: copper wire from electrical cable
Piercing saw and blades, round file
Necklace fastenings
*(See the **How to begin** chapter pages 12 to 23 for details on saws and files.)*

Ways of decorating tubing:

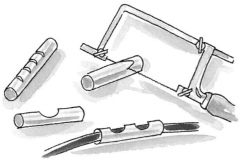

Tubing can be filed across its length with a round file until a hole appears. This can then be smoothed by running a file round the outline of the hole.

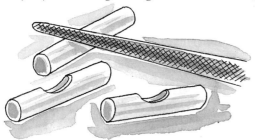

Holes can also be made by sawing into the tube at an angle from opposite sides. A series of straight cuts can also be used as a decorative effect. You can use cut tubes as a feature in their own right, or as an ornate way of lengthening a necklace; anything passing through the tube will be visible, so this can be used to great effect in a design.

Red amber beads with gold tubing

This is a good way to space large, graduated beads, where other beads cannot be found to enhance their shape or color.

REQUIREMENTS
Seventeen red amber oval beads graduating in size from 2.5 cm (1 in) to 1.3 cm (½ in)
Sixteen gold metal tubes 4 mm (⅕ in) diameter and 1 cm (⅜ in) long
Thin red cord 1 m (39 in) long
Wire, 0.8 mm (0.03 in) diameter, 15 cm (5⅞ in) long
Screw catch fastener

Making the necklace:
1 Sort out the beads in pairs of matching sizes, keeping the largest one for the center. Thread the largest bead on to the center of the cord and knot each side of the bead.
2 Add one metal tube to each side and knot. Continue to alternate the red beads and tubing, knotting each one and graduating the size of the red beads from the largest at the front to the smallest at the back, and ending with a metal tube. Tie a knot in the cord.
3 Cut a fine wire in half. At one end of each half, tie a single knot in the wire using pliers. If this is difficult make a small loop. Slide the hollow screw catch halves on to each wire so that the knot or loop sits inside the catch, and cut off any excess wire.

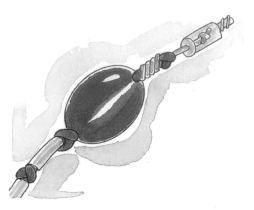

REQUIREMENTS
Three silver arrow head shaped beads
*   3.8 cm (1½ in) long*
Two silver patterned tube beads 2.5 cm
*   (1 in) long*
Silver tubing 4 mm diameter, 7.6 cm (3 in)
Silver tubing 3 mm diameter, 8 cm (3⅛ in)
Copper wire 1 mm diameter, 60 cm (23 in)
Silver chain 12.8 cm (5 in)
Bolt ring and loop
Round nosed pliers, wire cutters, round and
*   flat file, saw and sawblades*

4 Pass the remaining wire through the two end knots on the cord, then twist it four or five times round the cord, between the knot and the red bead. Tuck any remaining wire down through the beads, and cut off any excess close to a bead.

Arrow head necklace with silver tubing

Making the necklace:
1 Begin by sawing the tubing into the required lengths. Flatten off each end smoothly with a flat file.
2 Use a round file to file holes into the tubing pieces. Start slowly, and continue until the holes are a good size. Make two holes in the longer pieces of tube, and one in the four shortest lengths. Make all the holes the same size, and file the edges smooth.

3 Pass the copper wire through the beads and tubing one at a time, leaving 1 cm (⅜ in) at each side before cutting off. Bend the excess over with round nosed pliers to make loops at each end of the beads and tubes. Use the remaining length of copper wire to make twelve jump rings.
4 Link the beads together with the jump rings. Place one arrow head at the center, and a patterned tube bead each side. Follow this with arrow heads, then link on a long tube, followed by two short tubes.
5 Cut the chain in half, attaching each half to the last tube units with jump rings. Add the bolt ring fastener to each end. The necklace will be about 45 cm (18 in) long.

Unusual, arrow head beads are the focal point of this design. You could substitute any boldly shaped metal pendant beads.

Red amber beads blend well with matching cord and shiny gold tubing. The metallic arrow head necklace demonstrates a subtle use of different colored metals.

> **Note:** *Search for different metal objects to use as substitutes for beads. (You can drill through them to make pendants.) You may find that specialist electrical or plumbing suppliers and hobby shops can be the source of interesting materials.*

Natural form necklaces

These design ideas come directly from the materials themselves. Beach and country walks, as well as the kitchen or garden can provide interesting shells, pebbles, fragments of wood, fruit kernels and seeds. To these you can add complementary beads and other more exotic materials.

REQUIREMENTS
Natural forms: shells, cork, driftwood, fruit kernels, coffee beans, dried seeds etc.
Wooden shapes; rings and beads
Stone: soft stone, slate, amber, bone, horn
Leather thong: round and flat, or twine or raffia
Hand drill, needle drill with 1 mm bit
Files
Paints, varnish (optional)
Necklace fastenings (optional)
*(See the **How to begin** chapter pages 13 and 16 for information on drills and working with different materials.)*

Working with natural forms:
Sea shells may be used in many ways; one single, beautiful shell on twine or leather can be bold and striking, whereas lots of small shells strung together create a quite different, more delicate effect. A very large shell can have a bellcap finding glued to the tip, and this can then be worn on a thong or chain by attaching a jump ring.

Use stones in the same way as shells. To make simple design statements, try grouping small stones in clusters, mixed with beads and other forms to enhance their coloring. Stones can be difficult to drill, but softer stones like slate and sandstone can be worked successfully. Remember, these materials can also be tied into a necklace if drilling is not possible.

Bone and horn beads blend well with roughly shaped pieces of wood or stone, and you can incorporate these materials in their natural state, again by drilling or tying.

Cork (wine corks are useful) can be sliced easily with a sharp knife, or pierced with a skewer or a drill.

Fruit kernels, sea shells, pieces of cork and fragments of stone are just some of the natural forms you can use to make necklaces. Team these with leather thong and toning beads in subtle colors for the best effect.

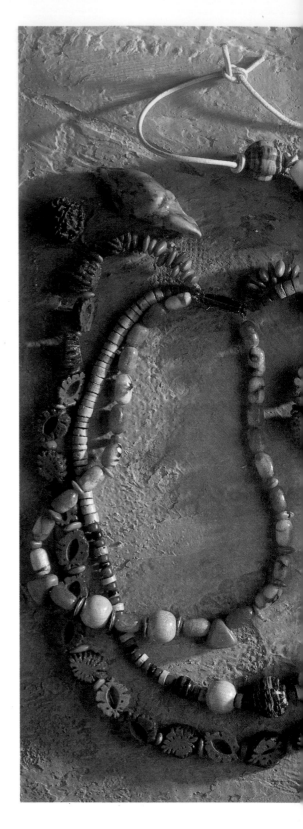

Shells and wooden hoop on thong

The shell colors are complemented by the limed wood hoop and the cream thong. To copy the effect, substitute your own shells and aim for the same color and weight balance as shown here.

REQUIREMENTS
Limed wood hoop 5.5 cm (2⅛ in) diameter
Two shells: one flat oval shell 6 cm (2⅜ in) long, and one conical shell 5 cm (2 in) long
Four striped wood beads 16 mm (⅝ in) diameter
Two drilled cork discs 2.5 cm (1 in) diameter
Two bone tube beads 5 cm (2 in) long
Hand or electric drill with 2.5 mm drill bit
1 m (39 in) cream round leather thong

Making the necklace:

1 Begin by drilling the shells and cork to allow the leather thong to pass through the drilled hole. Re-drill the bead holes if necessary to accommodate this.
2 Position the two drilled shells centrally on the leather thong, leaving a 4 cm (1½ in) gap between the two. Knot the thong to the wooden hoop as follows: pass the ends of the thong through the hoop from front to back. Pass the ends behind the top of the hoop and back through the space between the two shells at the front. Pull tightly so that the shells sit against the hoop neatly and the thong is looped through itself.
3 Leaving a 4 cm (1½ in) gap on the thong each side of the hoop, knot on a striped wooden bead, keeping the sides symmetrical. Leave another gap of 5 cm (2 in) and knot on the cork discs. After this leave another 5 cm (2 in) gap and knot on first the bone tube beads, then the other striped wood beads. To fasten, knot the thong at the ends, or add small bead trims.

Variations:

Grey slate and amber tube beads combine well with gold ceramic discs on dark leather thong. Gold paint colors a central stone disc and highlights the edges of the pendant.

Peach kernels and wooden beads make up a three strand necklace, strung on nylon gut and fastened with a triple loop clasp. To use kernels, saw them into slices, then drill and varnish them to provide a sheen.

Large beads on knotted thong

Heavy and ornate beads, particularly chunky, hand painted or 'ethnic' style beads can be made into necklaces by threading them on to leather thong. This is available as round or flat section thong, in a variety of colors and thicknesses to complement different color beads.

A combination of pale colors, carving, metallic finishes and inlays can result in a light, subtly intricate necklace, which can be enhanced by the use of white or cream leather thong. Similarly, a pleasing 'chunky' look can be achieved by combining large, coordinating ceramic beads in various sizes

with a toning thong. For a bright 'ethnic' style, vivid ceramic and hand-painted beads can be teamed with complementary or contrasting colored thong, and several rows can be worn together.

As with all the necklaces shown in this chapter, take the combinations of bead styles and their colors and sizes as a guide for creating your own designs. Be ready to experiment; these designs are easy to change.

Large ceramic beads painted with bold colorful patterns, and silver beads inlaid with bone suggest a strong ethnic influence. Each design is strung with a simple, complementary colored leather thong.

REQUIREMENTS
Beads and leather thong
Necklace fastenings

Tying knots in leather thong:

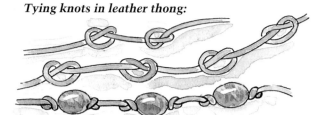

Use a basic single knot to hold a bead in place. Cross the thong over itself to form a loop, and pull it tight. The beads will often

'sit' better on the thong if the direction in which the knots are tied is alternated; for the first knot, loop the thong over the front then pull the end through the loop from back to front. Pass a bead on to the thong and, for the second knot loop the thong behind itself and pull the end through the loop from front to back. Continue in this way until all the beads are threaded.

To ensure the beads 'sit' well and are not knotted too tightly, stretch the knotted thong by pulling at it gently as you work. Always stretch the thong after each knot.

> **Note:** *Fastenings can be lace crimps with a screw catch, a bolt ring and hook, or you can make a fastening with round wire and pliers. (If using wire to make a fastening you will require a forming rod the same diameter as the leather thong – use wire or a nail for this – and epoxy resin or instant bonding glue.)*

Tie fastenings:
You can make a feature of the thong fastening by arranging the ends as bead-trimmed ties which hang down at the back of the neck. Allow extra thong length for this and check that any central beads are hanging correctly before knotting the beads in position. As the continual tying and untying of knots can crack the coating on colored thong, it is a good idea to use a natural leather shade for this style of fastening.

Crimp fastenings:

There are two main styles of crimp fastenings: those with screw ends, or those with a bolt hook and ring. To fit either, push each end of the thong into the tubular end of the crimp, and squeeze the tube gently with pliers so it grips the leather. (A lace crimp will fit the end of most round thongs.) Attach a screw fastener, or a bolt hook and ring to the crimp loops as desired.

Coil hook and loop fastenings:
You can make hook and loop ends for the thong from two lengths of wire twisted into coils over a forming rod. This rod can be a length of thick wire, or a nail with a diameter a little larger than the thong. Use chain nosed pliers to hold a wire on the forming rod and coil the wire tightly round until it is about 1–1.5 cm (⅜–⅝ in) long, or longer if the necklace is very heavy. Use round nosed pliers to bend the excess wire at the end of the coil into a hook shape. Make another coil with the other wire length, and bend the end into a loop. Cut any excess away with wire cutters. Spread a little instant bonding glue on the thong ends and twist the coils over this. Squeeze them tightly with chain nosed pliers to 'bite' on to the leather thong.

Cream and silver bead necklace

Ornate silver beads are combined with toning bone and porcelain beads to make a richly textured but subtle necklace design. The pale colors are complemented by white leather thong.

REQUIREMENTS:

Three large silver colored, decorative beads 35 mm (1⅜ in) diameter, inlaid with circles of mother of pearl

Two lightly carved cream porcelain beads 25 mm (1 in) diameter

Two bone beads inlaid with metal strips 22 mm (⅞ in) diameter

Two silver colored decorative beads 18 mm (¾ in) diameter

Two lightly carved bone tube beads 30 mm (1¼ in) long

Two bone grooved tube beads 30 mm (1¼ in) long

Two silver ornate tube beads 25 mm (1 in) long

Four small silver beads 8 mm (³⁄₁₆ in) diameter

Coil ends for fastening or 18 cm (7 in) length 1.2 mm (0.05 in) diameter round silver wire

White leather thong 2 mm diameter, 1.5 m (1⅝ yd)

Round nosed pliers, chain nosed pliers, wire cutters

Making the necklace:

1 Start with one of the large silver disc beads and slide it on to the middle of the thong. Knot the thong close to the bead at each side. Add the beads as follows, keeping each side the same and knotting the thong at each side of the beads in alternate directions to keep them in place.

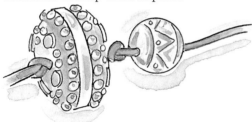

2 Next to the central decorative silver bead add a cream porcelain bead, then another decorative silver bead. Leave a gap of 2.5 cm (1 in) on the thong before knotting into place a small silver bead. Add the round bone metal inlaid bead, then the silver ornate round bead. Again leave a gap of 2.5 cm (1 in) on the thong before knotting on another of the small silver beads, followed by a carved bone tube and the grooved bone tube. Knot this in place leaving 15 mm (⅝ in) of thong.

3 Make coil hook and loop fastenings from two 9 cm (3½ in) lengths of 1.2 mm diameter silver wire, as previously decribed.

Variations:

Patterned ceramic beads can be teamed with plain toning beads, and knotted close together on cream thong to create a necklace like the cream and pink design shown here. Add fastenings as desired.

Beads with a strong color theme like terracotta, cream and black are used here to make a necklace. Choose beads with coordinating patterns like these round and tube-shaped designs, and knot them on to natural leather thong as this complements their warm coloring.

One large patterned bead knotted centrally on a dark leather thong, and spaced with two toning beads on each side creates a simple but effective design. Tie the long thong ends to make a choker-style necklace, or adjust the length as desired, perhaps adding beads to the ends as a back view feature to complement an outfit.

Buying beads

When buying beads or thongs, always check that the holes drilled through the beads are large enough for the leather thong to pass through. Also, try to find a supplier who sells thong by the meter (yard). Ready cut lengths are often too short for projects where much knotting is required between the beads.

Twisted wire links and beads

Necklaces made with these materials offer endless design opportunities as the designs can be altered dramatically just by changing the size and shape of the chain or individual links, or the position of the beads.

A chain can be made from equal size metal links, or by graduating their size so larger links are at the front, and smaller links are at the back. Beads can be positioned anywhere along this chain. Links can be made from different colored metals, so a design could incorporate gold, silver, brass and copper wire, or be made from any one of these. The appearance of the links can also be changed dramatically by flattening them with a hammer.

Beads can be chosen to complement the sparkling color of the wire, or to act as a contrast. Large or very brightly patterned beads always tend to be the focus of attention, while smaller beads can be used to balance the impact of large or decorative links. They can also be added to fine wire links to create delicate effects which contrast or tone with the wire.

REQUIREMENTS
Metal wire
Jump rings
Round nosed pliers
Wire cutters
A flat metal file
*(See the **How to Begin** chapter page 16 for how to make jump rings)*

Making a template:

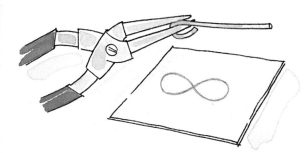

Draw the exact size and shape of link you require on to paper, to use as a pattern template. Make two links by twisting the wire to shape with chain nosed pliers, and checking the shape against the drawing as you work. Cut the link from the strip of wire when the shape is correct. Keep one link as a reference for the others, and straighten the second one out completely. This will show you the length of wire needed to make each link.

A figure eight link:

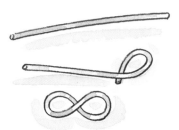

Using a template as a guide, cut a length of wire to the required size. File the cut ends flat to neaten. Twist one end of the wire with the round nosed pliers until it touches the middle point of the wire length. Use the pliers again to bend the other end of the wire in the opposite direction to make a figure eight shape.

Curled link variations:

Curled links, which are variations of a figure eight shape, are easy to form with round nosed pliers. Work to a pattern template for speed and accuracy.

Twisted wire links manage to create a delicate effect, even when not made from very fine wire. These necklace designs work well because the colors and the shapes of the beads are in harmony.

Making links through beads:

Cut a wire longer than the bead, and pass it through the bead leaving about 1 cm (³⁄₈ in) at each end. Use round nosed pliers to bend these ends into loops, twisting them slightly to secure. If the hole in the bead is large enough, tuck the end of the wire loop back into the bead.

Joining links to bead loops:

Use round nosed pliers to open the metal link slightly, then slip it over the loop at the end of the bead. Make sure that the bead cannot slip off by closing the link carefully. If the links are not secure, the necklace will remain in place while being worn, but may fall apart when stored flat.

> **Note:** *You could adapt any of the twisted link necklaces here by changing the color scheme dramatically, and substituting gold or copper colored wire with toning beads – or a mixture of different color beads – for the versions shown here. You could also try linking multiple groups of links together, or making a tassel from lengths of different colored metal chain.*

Turquoise bead necklace with silver links

Create this stylish tassel-trimmed necklace with decorative turquoise colored pottery beads spaced between silver colored beads and curled links.

REQUIREMENTS

*Five round turquoise 'verdigris' effect
    pottery beads 20 mm (³⁄₄ in) diameter
Ten matching flat cushion beads 12 mm
    (¹⁄₂ in) diameter
Six silver beads 18 mm (⁵⁄₈ in) diameter
One silver bead 7 mm (³⁄₁₀ in) diameter
Silver curb chain 70 cm (³⁄₄ yd) length
Silver wire 11cm (¹⁄₈ yd) × 1mm diameter
Silver wire 140 cm (55 in) × 1.2 mm
    diameter
Silver wire 60 cm (23¹⁄₂ in) × 0.8 mm
    diameter
Hook and ring fastening, round nosed
    pliers, snub nosed pliers, wire cutters,
    flat metal file*

Making the links:
1   Cut the 1.2 mm wire into twenty 6 cm (2¼ in) lengths and shape them into twenty figure eight links. Make eight jump rings from the remainder of the wire, by cutting them from a coil shaped over a form with a 5 mm (³⁄₁₆ in) diameter.

2   Pass the 0.8 mm diameter wire through the silver colored beads, leaving 1 cm (³⁄₈ in) at each end, and bend these ends into loops. Tuck the wire ends back into the beads if possible. Thread the same diameter wire through the pottery beads, joining them into four units of three beads as follows: thread together two flat cushion beads with a larger, round bead in the center. Twist the wire ends into loops.

Making the tassel:

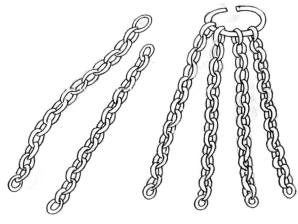

1   Cut the curb chain into ten 7 cm (2¾ in) lengths. Pass 3 cm (1¼ in) of the 1 mm wire through the end links of the chains. Bend the wire into a tight circle, twisting the wire ends together so that the chains hang in a neat tassel. Cut off any excess wire and tuck the twisted wire ends down so that they are hidden by the hanging chains.

2   Take 8 cm (3¼ in) of the 1 mm wire and make a loop at one end. Pass a 7 mm (³⁄₁₀ in) diameter silver colored bead on to the wire so that it sits on the loop. Place this bead and wire inside the chain tassel and pass the wire up through the center of the tassel. (The bead inside will help the chains to sit evenly against the pottery beads.)

Joining the tassel, beads and links:
1   Pass the wire from the tassel through the three remaining pottery beads, following the sequence one flat, one large round, one flat, as before. Form a secure loop from the remaining wire.
2   Add a jump ring to the tassel bead unit, then add two figure eight links to this. These form the beginnings of the sides of the necklace. Continue in the following order: silver colored bead, figure eight link, pottery bead unit, figure eight link, silver colored bead.
3   After the last silver colored bead has been added, complete the necklace by adding a figure eight link to each one, then add the remainder of these figure eight links each side of the necklace, joining each one with a jump ring. Finish off with a jump ring and attach the hook and ring fastening.

Variations:
Oval clear glass beads and silver colored wire create a subtle effect. Join small, tubular beads each side of seven large glass beads with links and loops, and join these to decorative curled links with jump rings.

Richly patterned glass beads can be joined with delicately proportioned curled links made from toning colored wire. Fit a ready-made decorative finding – chosen in a color to match the links, and in a style to complement – on each side of the bead.

Multiple bead necklaces

These timeless necklaces can look really sophisticated or fairly casual depending on the choice of beads. The designs can be ornate, with bright or patterned beads and gold bead caps on a gold chain, or low key with subtle, plain or pearlized beads linked to a matt metal chain.

The length of the necklace is a personal choice, but take the weight of the beads into consideration when deciding on this. Glass beads for example are heavy, so these would be best mixed with other, lighter varieties.

You will find these necklaces are very easy to make, although they are more time consuming than other projects.

REQUIREMENTS
Beads and bead caps (optional)
Metal chain
Headpins (short length)
Round nosed pliers
Wire cutters
Necklace fastener
(See the How to begin chapter pages 16 to
*   18 for details on beads, headpins and*
*   fastenings)*

Looping the beads:

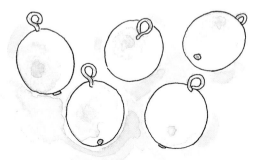

When starting a project, sort out the beads in sizes, and prepare them all with headpins. Pass the headpin through the bead (or the bead cap followed by the bead and another bead cap). Leave 1 cm (⅜ in) above the bead and cut off any excess. Twist the wire into a loop with round nosed pliers.

Attaching beads to chain:
Using pliers, twist the loop on the beads open slightly, then close it over a link on the chain. Vary the position of the beads on the chain; do not have them all hanging in one direction.

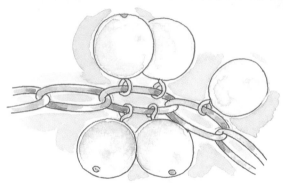

Lay the chain flat as you work, and attach beads at the top and the base of the links to vary their effect. Depending on their size, you may have three or four beads on one link; check the effect.

Fastenings:
Any type of necklace fastening can be used. If the loops on the chain are not open, use jump rings to attach the fastener to the chain. In some chain links you may be able to open the last link to make a hook. Do this only if you think it will be a secure fastening.

Cream and grey pearl necklace
Cream 'pearls' and grey pearlized beads create a classic combination – on humble hardware chain.

REQUIREMENTS
Forty 15 mm (⁹⁄₁₆ in) diameter drilled pearls
Sixty 8 mm (⁵⁄₁₆ in) diameter dark grey
*   pearls*
One hundred 4 cm (1½ in) silver headpins
Matt silver grey hardware chain 46 cm
*   (18 in)*
Round nosed pliers, wire cutters

Making the necklace:
1   Prepare all the beads on the headpins, and form loops on the ends.
2   Attach the pearls evenly along the chain, varying their position on the links.
3   Attach the grey pearls amongst the pearls, ensuring that the chain is well covered.
4   Fix a fastener to the ends of the chain, or make the last link into a hook if the chain is suitable for this.

Differently sized grey and cream pearls are linked to silver chain to create this classic choker-style necklace. When worn, all the pearls 'sit' in the right direction.

Chapter 5
Jewelry sets

Jewelry sets allow the wearer to mix or match individual pieces to complement particular items of clothing. A necklace with matching earrings or with a brooch or hairclip makes a definite statement; they emphasize the color theme of the materials used, the clothing, or both.

When making a piece of jewelry it is always wise to allow for enough extra materials to make a matching piece. For example, if you are making a necklace, buy extra chain, beads and stones so that you can make a bracelet or earrings at a later date. There is nothing more frustrating than not being able to obtain the same link of chain, or color of beads as previously used.

Most of the techniques used in this chapter are covered in the **'How to begin'** chapter, or in individual projects involving similar materials. Those that are not are explained in the project instructions.

Pearls and crystals

Pearls and crystals always look good together. Because this combination is very adaptable, the jewelry can be worn in a formal or more casual way; they can look equally good with jeans and sweater as with a smart cocktail or party dress.

Bracelet and drop earrings

REQUIREMENTS
For the bracelet:
Eight 1.8 cm ($^{11}/_{16}$ in) pearl beads
Eight 9 mm ($^{5}/_{16}$ in) crystal beads
Silver threading wire to fit beads
Two small silver jump rings
One 4 mm ($^{2}/_{16}$ in) silver jump ring
One silver bolt ring
For the earrings:
Two 2.5 cm (1 in) flat backed pearl domes
Four 1.8 cm ($^{11}/_{16}$ in) pearl beads
Two 6 mm ($^{3}/_{16}$ in) crystals
Two 5 cm (2 in) silver headpins
Two flat plate earring fittings with loop (or
without loop, use a hand drill with
0.8 mm drill bit and 0.8 mm wire to
make pegs and loops)
Pliers, wire cutters, instant bonding glue

The classic designs here have a timeless appeal. They are: a pearl and crystal bracelet with drop earrings, a multi-pearl bracelet and earrings, and a pearl and crystal drop necklace and earrings.

Making the bracelet:

1 Starting with a pearl, pass the silver wire through the pearls and crystals, alternating them as you thread.

2 Wind the ends of the wire around the small jump rings three times, then pass the end of the wire back through the last pearl.

3 Attach a larger ring, and the bolt ring to the end jump rings.

Making the earrings:

1 For each earring, pass the headpin through a pearl, followed by a crystal, and a pearl. Loop the end of the headpin, and cut off any excess wire.

2 If using clip-on fittings with a loop, glue these to the flat back of the pearl dome, so that the loop protrudes at the edge.

3 If attaching fittings for pierced ears, glue these a little above the center back to prevent the earrings from falling forward when worn. Drill into the bottom edge of each pearl dome for 5 mm (³/₁₆ in). Make a loop from wire with a 5 mm (³/₁₆ in) peg, and glue this into each drilled hole.

4 To assemble each earring, attach the drop pearl and crystal unit to the loop on the pearl dome earring fitting.

Multi-pearl bracelet and earrings

This is similar to the necklace shown in the **Necklaces** chapter, but the gold chain used here gives the design a more traditional look. Try mixing white and cream pearls with the crystals, to add subtle depths.

REQUIREMENTS
For the bracelet:
Thirty five pearl beads between 1 cm (³/₈ in) and 1.2 cm (⁷/₁₆ in) diameter
Seven oval crystals 1.2 cm (⁷/₁₆ in) diameter
Forty two gold headpins
Gold curb chain 18 cm (7 in) long
Gold bracelet fastening: bolt ring and loop
For the earrings:
Two 6 cm (2⁵/₁₆ in) lengths of gold curb chain
Eight 8 mm (⁵/₁₆ in) diameter pearl beads
Four 10 mm (³/₈ in) diameter pearl beads
Two 12 mm (⁷/₁₆ in) diameter pearl beads
Four oval crystals 8 mm (⁵/₁₆ in) long
Two oval crystals (10 mm (³/₈ in) long
Gold earring fittings and two gold jump rings
Twenty gold headpins
Pliers and wire cutters
*(See the **Necklaces** chapter, page 76 for details on looping the beads and attaching them to chain.)*

Making the bracelet:

1 Lay the curb chain flat on the work surface. Thread each pearl on to a headpin, and attach them evenly along the chain. Start with the larger pearls and attach them to both sides of the links. Check that the chain looks evenly covered.

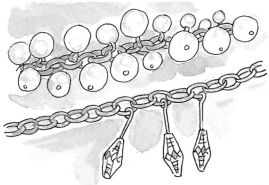

2 Attach the crystals in the same way, but leave the headpins longer so that the crystals hang down below the pearls. Arrange them on the chain so that they will all hang down in the same direction when worn. Check to see the effect.

3 Finish off the bracelet by attaching a bolt ring to one end of the chain, and a loop to the other end.

Making the earrings:
1 For each earring, join the ends of each length of chain together with a jump ring. Attach an earring fitting to the jump ring.
2 Hold up the chain loop to find the center front link. Thread a large pearl on to a headpin and loop this on to the center link. Distribute the other threaded pearls symmetrically on the chain.

3 Attach the crystals, arranging the larger one at the center front, next to the larger pearl, and the smaller ones next to the middle-sized pearls.

Pearl and crystal set
Here the focus of the necklace is on the crystal drop at the front. The pearl drop earrings are a simple complementary design.

REQUIREMENTS
For the necklace:
One large oval crystal drop 3.2 cm (1¼ in) long
One oval crystal bead 2 cm (¾ in) long
Ten 12 mm (⁷⁄₁₆ in) diameter crystal beads
Ten 8 mm (⁵⁄₁₆ in) diameter pearl beads
Twenty 9 mm (³⁄₈ in) diameter crystal beads
One large silver clawed bellcap
Two silver calotte crimps
Silver bolt ring, jump ring and eyepin
Synthetic thread and threading needle
For the earrings:
Two 12 mm (⁷⁄₁₆ in) pearl drops
Two 10 mm (³⁄₈ in) pearl beads
Two 8 mm (⁵⁄₁₆ in) crystal beads
Two silver pegged cups
Four silver eyepins
Two silver earring fittings
Pliers, wire cutters, instant bonding glue

Making the necklace:
1 Take a length of doubled thread on a threading needle, and pass two of the smaller pearls to the center on the thread. (If the holes in the beads are not so large that the knot would disappear inside, knot between each bead.)
2 To each side of these two center pearls add beads symmetrically in the following order: a crystal, a large pearl, a crystal, a smaller pearl, a crystal, a large pearl and so on until all the beads are used. ◄
3 At the end of the threaded beads, tie a double reef knot as close as possible to the last bead. To this fasten a calotte crimp and cut off the excess thread. Do this to both ends, then attach a jump ring to one end and a bolt ring to the other.
4 To make the crystal drop, glue the clawed bellcap to the top of the crystal drop. The claws will open up to sit neatly on the crystal. Attach an eyepin to the bellcap and pass the oval crystal bead on to this eyepin.

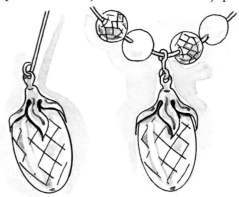

5 Loop the top of the eyepin on to the necklace between the two center front pearls. Close the loop to the crystal drop.

Making the earrings:

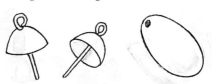

1 Glue the pegged cap to the drop pearls.
2 For each earring, attach an eyepin to the peg cap, and pass on a pearl bead. Loop the end of the eyepin.
3 Attach a second eyepin to this loop and pass on a crystal bead. Loop the top of the eyepin and attach the earring fittings.

Safety pin jewelry

Safety pins have been used to make innovative jewelry for decades, but they came to the fore most recently in the 'punk' movement, when they were used to make simple chains and earrings. Here they are used in a discreet way – in fact it is not immediately noticeable that the materials used include safety pins.

Different pins:

If possible, try to use small copper safety pins, which may be available from notions departments and craft stores. These are ideal for making jewelry, as the color is a good contrast for many beads. Brass safety pins also complement beads well, and are preferable to ordinary chrome pins which do not create such an attractive effect, being rather large.

Packs of pins usually include mixed sizes. Small size pins are best for necklaces and earrings, while medium sizes are good for making bracelets. However, all the sizes can be used, so keep them in supply.

Beads and thread:

Bugle beads, rocaille beads and other small beads threaded on to safety pins transform their appearance with a variety of color and shaded effects. The pins themselves look attractive threaded on gold elastic, but if this is unobtainable, use black or white round elastic instead.

Threading the pins:

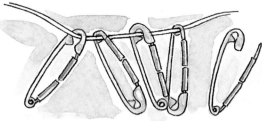

Thread each pin with beads before stringing on elastic. (Check that the pin is securely closed, and squeeze the head with pliers if necessary.) Thread the beaded pins on to

Small copper and gold safety pins provide the base for these impressive designs. The collars and matching earrings are decorated with bugle beads, and the clips and bangles are trimmed with small, round beads.

elastic in alternate order: through the head of one beaded pin first, then through the hole at the base of the next pin. If you are color grading the beads, make sure to thread the pins accordingly, so that the color sequence is the same way up once the pins are threaded. Also, make sure that the beads on the pins are all lying at the same side – facing towards the front of the piece – check this carefully each time by placing them on a flat surface.

Pin and bead collar and earrings

This set has a substantial look to it, despite being made up of so many small units. The color mix of gold and silver adds depth and dimension to the design.

REQUIREMENTS
For the necklace:
One hundred and ten small brass safety pins
Eighty five medium brass safety pins
Silver bugle beads
Gold bugle beads
Fine round elastic (to fit through the hole in the pin head), 43 cm (17 in) long
Two gold calotte crimps, screw necklace fastening
For the earrings:
Six medium brass safety pins
Two small brass safety pins
Two 10 mm (⁴/₁₀ in) hoops made from 0.8 mm gold wire
Two gold fish hook earring fittings
Pliers

Making the necklace:
1 Take the elastic and knot one end. Attach a calotte crimp to this knot.
2 Bead the safety pins with bugle beads. The medium pins take three bugle beads, and the smaller pins two beads. Bead twenty two medium pins with gold beads and sixty three medium pins with silver beads. Of the smaller pins, bead seventy two with gold beads, and thirty eight with silver beads.
3 Arrange the beaded pins on elastic as follows: pass on seventeen of the small gold beaded pins. Follow this with thirty eight small pins beaded alternately with gold and silver beads. (Keep checking that the beads are all facing the same way, and that the pin heads and bases are threaded alternately.)

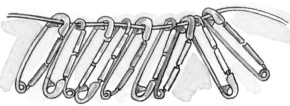

4 Now add the larger pins. Start with a gold beaded pin, followed by three silver beaded pins, then another gold beaded pin. Thereafter, every fourth pin should be gold and the others silver. Continue in this sequence until all eighty five pins are used.
5 Now return to the smaller pins. The first thirty eight of these should alternate gold and silver beads, followed by the last seventeen pins which have all gold beads.
6 After the last pin is threaded, tie a knot in the elastic and add the other calotte crimp. Do not stretch the elastic, because tight elastic would prevent the pins from 'sitting' well. The pins may appear to lie in all directions at this point, but they will fall into place when worn.
7 Attach the necklace fastening to the calotte crimps.

Making the earrings:
1 With the 0.8 mm wire make two hoops with 1 cm (⅜ in) diameters.
2 Bead the larger pins; four with gold beads, and two with silver beads. Bead the two small pins with silver beads.
3 To each hoop add one small pin and three larger ones, alternating the color of the beads. Thread the hoop alternately through the top and the base of the pins, as for threading the necklace.

4 Attach the earring fittings to the hoops, ensuring that the beads are hanging to the front, and that the earrings have been made in mirror image: both small pins to either the inside or the outside of the hoop.

Blue beaded pin choker and earrings

The combination of iridescent blue beads and brass pins gives this design a certain Egyptian quality. For the necklace, the pins are threaded on to a thin gold wire, which is joined to a gold chain. The earrings are a simple design linked to a gold ring.

REQUIREMENTS
For the choker:
34 cm (13½ in) 1.0 mm diameter gold wire
14 cm (5½ in) gold curb chain
Thirty seven medium size brass safety pins
Twenty four small brass safety pins
Iridescent blue bugle beads (each medium size pin is threaded with three beads, and each small pin is threaded with two beads)
Twelve 5 mm (³/₁₆ in) iridescent blue rocaille beads
Eighteen 5 mm (³/₁₆ in) gold beads
Twenty one 4 mm (¹/₅ in) gold beads
Twenty four 3 mm (¹/₈ in) gold beads
Screw necklace fastening
For the earrings:
Four medium size brass safety pins
Iridescent blue bugle beads (three for each pin)
Two 5 mm (³/₁₆ in) gold beads
Two 3 mm (¹/₈ in) gold beads
Two hoops 1 cm (³/₈ in) diameter 0.8 mm gold wire
Two gold fish hook earring fitting
Pliers and wire cutters

Making the necklace:

1 Begin by twisting the end of the wire into a small loop. To the other end add the beads and beaded pins as follows: (Check that the wire is threaded through the pins through the head and base alternately, and that all the beads face the same side.) Firstly, thread on nine of the 5 mm (³/₁₆ in) gold beads. Follow this with one of the small beaded pins, and alternate twelve of these with twelve 3 mm (¹/₈ in) gold beads.

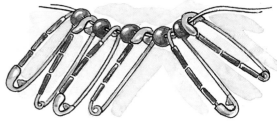

2 Next add one of the larger beaded pins and alternate six of these with five 4 mm (¹/₅ in) gold beads. After the last pin add a blue rocaille bead, a larger pin, a 4 mm (¹/₅ in) gold bead, and so on until the rocaille beads are all used.
3 Continue alternating the remaining larger pins with the remaining 4 mm (¹/₅ in) gold beads. Next alternate the remaining twelve smaller pins with the twelve 3 mm (¹/₈ in) gold beads. Finally, add the other nine 5 mm (³/₁₆ in) gold beads and twist the end of the wire into a loop. Cut off any excess.

4 At each end of the wire attach half of the gold chain to the loop, and attach the screw fastenings to the other ends. Bend the necklace gently to shape to ensure a good fit round the neck.

Making the earrings:
1 Make two hoops 1 cm (³/₈ in) diameter with 0.8 mm wire.
2 To each hoop add one of the 3 mm (¹/₈ in) gold beads, followed by a small beaded pin,

two of the larger beaded pins and then a 5 mm (³⁄₁₆ in) gold bead. Ensure that the earrings are a mirror image of each other.
3   Add the earring fittings to the hoop.

Variations:
Change the earring design by adding more pins for a chunky effect, or create a drop effect by adding a double row of pins.

Safety pin bracelets and hairclips
These bracelets are shown with different beads and color schemes to illustrate the various design options. They can of course be made to match a necklace and earrings.

If you have some pins and beads left over you can use them to decorate a hairclip in the same way. As for the bracelet sizes, adjust the numbers of beads and pins as required for your design.

REQUIREMENTS
For a bracelet:
Fifty large or forty four medium size brass or copper safety pins
Three 5 mm (³⁄₁₆ in) rocaille or clear glass beads for each pin
Round elastic 2 mm (¹⁄₁₆ in) diameter 44 cm (17¼ in) long
For a hairclip:
A flat metal hairclip 6 cm (2⁵⁄₁₆ in) long
Fourteen large brass or copper safety pins
Three beads 5 mm (³⁄₁₆ in) diameter for each safety pin
Round elastic

Making the bracelets:
1   Cut the elastic in half. Thread the beaded pins alternately through the head and base on to one piece of elastic. When all the pins are threaded, tie a secure knot close to the pins, to form a circle of beaded pins.
2   Thread the other piece of elastic through the other ends of the pins, and tie a knot to secure as before. Check that both elastic lengths are equal length, and trim excess.

Making the hairclip:
1   Tie a small knot in the elastic. Thread on the beaded pins alternately through head and base. Tie a knot in the elastic close to the last pin and cut off any excess. Repeat for the other end of the pin.
2   Slide this beaded unit on to the hairclip so that the bar of the clip sits inside the unbeaded sides of the pins.

Padded fabric jewelry

The success of this jewelry depends on the choice of fabric or ribbon. Small pattern repeats work best, and firmly woven evening fabrics with a little glitter thread are ideal. Experiment to find the best effects.

You can also make this jewelry using 'friendly plastic' material; experiment with circles, triangles and squares as these are easy-to-handle shapes.

Suitable adhesives:
The edges of the folded fabrics are stuck together, but finding the best glue for the fabric is also a matter for experiment. Instant bonding glue works well with some fabrics, while others stick better with epoxy resin adhesive. All adhesives should be used sparingly to avoid marking the fabric.

Padding the shapes:

A light filling of polyester batting is used to pad the shapes. Cut this to the same shape as the folded fabric, but a little smaller all round so that it fits within the glued edges of the covering fabric.

Waterproofing the jewelry:
Before attaching the jewelry findings, you can varnish the fabric shapes with medium or clear craft varnish. This will also help strengthen the fabric.

Attaching jewelry findings:

These are glued to the back of the shapes. For earrings, clip-on fastenings are the easiest to apply, as these are simple to stick in place. To attach loops or jump rings, first make a hole with a needle through the fabric and insert the fitting through this.

Dark tartan lapel pin and earrings

The set is made from five folded squares of fabric. Three of these are slipped on to a lapel pin, and the earring shapes are pierced through a corner, and hung from jump rings and pierced ear hooks.

REQUIREMENTS
Five 3.5 cm (1⅜ in) squares of taffeta ribbon
Scraps of lightweight batting
Suitable adhesive
A 9 cm (3½ in) lapel pin
Two jump rings and fish hook ear fittings

Making the triangles:
1 Cut a triangle of batting to fit inside the fabric, so that when the fabric is folded over into a triangle shape, a border of 5 mm (³⁄₁₆ in) is left all round for gluing.
2 Apply the glue sparingly to the edge of the wrong side of the fabric. Fold the square diagonally, placing the batting inside, and press the edges to stick.

3 Once the glue has dried, coat the shapes with varnish and leave to dry.

To make the pin:
Starting at the folded side of one triangle, thread the pin through the back, then repeat for two more triangles, overlapping each one slightly.

To make the earrings:
For each one, pierce through a corner, through the glued edge and insert a jump ring. Attach a fish hook fitting to each ring.

Variations:
A tartan ribbon brooch and earrings are made from slightly larger squares of taffeta ribbon. Glue a brooch pin centrally to the back of the large triangle, and glue clip-on earring fittings centrally on the backs of the smaller triangles. Align these so that the side of the clip fitting is parallel with the folded edge of the triangle.

Tartan ribbon is an ideal fabric for this style of jewelry, as the colors and scale complement the shapes so well.

Shell jewelry sets

You can develop a theme by choosing shells of the same color or shape. Take strong elements – one beautiful shell from the necklace for example, and use the same type of shells as the main feature in the earrings, or to make a matching bracelet.

Pendant shell necklace and earrings

This ornate set uses silver beads to enhance and contrast with the shiny shells. The design also includes shell slices and beads taken from discarded necklaces.

Remember, the threading order of the shells is given as a guide. As sizes and shapes vary you may have to add or subtract shells at one side of the central pendant shell to keep an even balance.

REQUIREMENTS
For the necklace:
One large spiral shell 6 cm (2⅜ in) long
One flat oval shell 5 cm (2 in) long
Fourteen 4 mm (⅕ in) shell beads
Ten varied shells in five matching pairs
Six patterned silver beads in three matching pairs, ranging in size from 1 cm (⅜ in) to 1.5 cm (⅝ in)
Four 8 mm (⁵⁄₁₆ in) shell beads
Six 1 cm (⅜ in) shell washers
Sixty four drilled curved shell slices
Two 8 mm (⁵⁄₁₆ in) silver beads
Twenty tubular 'liquid silver' twist beads
Two silver calotte crimps
One silver screw fastening
Two silver eyepins and six 4 mm (⅕ in) jump rings
Nylon thread (gut)
Pliers, wire cutters, drill and 1 mm drill bit
For the earrings:
Two oval flat shells 4.5 cm (1¾ in) long
Ten drilled curved shell pieces
Four tubular 'liquid silver' twist beads
Two long silver eyepins and jump rings
Two silver earring fittings
*(See the **How to begin** chapter page 19 for details on working with shells)*

Making the necklace:

1 Drill through all the shells and pass jump rings through any flat, more delicate shells. Attach a jump ring through one of the natural holes at the top of the large flat oval shell, and through the spiral shell if this is not too thick.

Otherwise, pass an eyepin through the spiral shell, loop it over inside, and loop the other end over a jump ring.

2 Drill a hole at the base of the flat oval shell. Pass an eyepin through this and loop it inside to secure. Loop the other end over the jump ring on the spiral shell.

3 Pass the nylon thread through the jump ring at the top of the flat oval shell. To each side of this add beads and shells in the following order: two 4 mm (³⁄₁₆ in) shell beads, eight curved shell slices, one drilled shell, three 4 mm (³⁄₁₆ in) shell beads, one flat shell with jump ring and one larger patterned silver bead.

4 Continue with eight curved shell slices, one 8 mm (⁵⁄₁₆ in) shell bead, a shell washer, 8 mm (⁵⁄₁₆ in) shell bead, two 4 mm (³⁄₁₆ in) shell beads, a flat shell with jump ring, a drilled spiral shell, eight curved shell slices, another drilled shell, eight curved shell slices, a patterned silver bead, shell washer, ten tubular silver twist beads.

5 At the ends of this, knot the nylon thread with a tight double knot and enclose each end in a calotte crimp. Attach a screw fastening to each crimp.

The earrings:

1 For each one, pass the jump ring through the natural hole in the flat oval shell.
2 To this attach a long eyepin and pass on ten drilled shell slices, followed by two silver tubular twist beads. Twist the other end of the eyepin into a loop. Attach an earring fitting to the loop.

Polished shells make spectacular jewelry. Here, similar tubular beads are used to complement their subtle coloring.

Further reading

There are numerous books and magazines available on making your own jewelry. Listed here are a few books on specific techniques and inspirational designs.

Coles, Janet & Robert Bydwig. *The Book of Beads*. New York: Simon & Schuster, 1990.
Dublin, Lois Sherr. *The History of Beads from 3,000 B.C. to the Present*. New York: Abrams, 1987.
Moss, Kathlyn, and Alice Scherer. *The New Beadwork*. New York: Abrams, 1992.
Poris, Ruth F. *Advanced Beadwork*. Tampa, Florida: Golden Hands Press, 1990.
—. *Step-by-Step Bead Stringing*. Tampa, Florida: Golden Hands Press, 1988.
Tomalin, Stefany. *Beads! Make your own unique jewellery*. New York: Sterling, 1992.

Useful addresses

Bead and jewelry supply stores have opened up around the country in recent years. You may find one in an urban area near you. The following is a short selection of mail order bead suppliers. You will find additional listings and advertisements in many craft magazines. One that is particularly helpful is *Ornament* (available at news-stands, by writing to P.O. Box 2349, San Marcos, CA 92079-2349, or by calling 1-800-888-8950). For a more extensive list, you may want to purchase the following publication, a comprehensive listing of bead suppliers in the U.S., Canada, and England. Send $14.95 plus $2.00 for shipping and handling to:
The Bead Directory
P.O. Box 10103
Oakland, CA 94610

Bead Bazaar
1345 Spruce Street
Boulder, Colorado 80302
(303) 444-8097
(Send $3 for current catalog.)

Beads Unique
308 Roberts Lane
Bakersfield, CA 93308
805-399-6523
(Wide variety of beads, tools, and books. Send $3.00 for current brochure.)

Garden of Beadin'
P. O. Box 1535
Redway, CA 95560
707-923-9120
(Large assortment of beads, supplies, and findings. Send $2.00 for current catalog.)

International Beadtrader Inc.
2750 South Broadway
Englewood, CO 80110
303-781-8335
(Beads, findings, supplies. Send $3.00 for catalog.)

KUMA Beads
P.O. Box 2719
Glenville, NY 12325
518-384-0110
(Beads, findings, tools, books, and jewelry supplies. Send $2.00 for a catalog.)

Shipwreck Beads
2727 Westmoor Ct. SW
Olympia, WA 98502
206-754-2323
(Thousands of imported glass beads. Send $3.00 for catalog.)

The Bead Shop
177 Hamilton Ave.
Palo Alto, CA 94301
415-828-7880
(Beads, kits, findings, books. Send $3.00 for catalog.)

The Nature Company
750 Hearst Ave.
Berkeley, CA 94710
1-800-227-1114
(Beads and supplies. Request catalog or store near you.)

TSI
101 Nickerson St.
P.O. Box 9266
Seattle, WA 89109
1-800-426-9984
(Jewelry-making supplies and tools.)

Index